MACAULAY

MACAULAY

◆

Arthur Bryant

BARNES & NOBLE

BOOKS

10 East 53d St., New York 10022

(a division of Harper & Row Publishers, inc.)

First published by Peter Davies in October 1932

Published in the U.S.A. 1979 by
HARPER & ROW PUBLISHERS, INC.
BARNES & NOBLE IMPORT DIVISION
ISBN 0–06–490761–9

Printed and bound in Great Britain by
Morrison & Gibb Ltd., London and Edinburgh

To
G. M. Trevelyan
Master of my Craft

'Of Macaulay, too, something must here be said, because an undistinguishing condemnation of him used to be the shibboleth of that school of English historians who destroyed the habit of reading history among their fellow-countrymen.'

G. M. TREVELYAN

Contents

Illustrations

Introduction to New Edition

THIS short life of Macaulay, long out of print, was written immediately after the completion of my first full length historical biography, *Charles II*. To its original hundred and sixty pages I have now added a further sixteen to bring my portrait of this great master of my craft into focus with the slightly wider vision I might have brought to it after half a lifetime of practising his craft. Yet, though there is a little I have been able to add to my miniature of close on half a century ago, I have found nothing to change in it.

My little book owed much to the generous help of G. M. Trevelyan – Macaulay's great-nephew – who not only encouraged me at every stage of its writing but allowed me the use of Macaulay's diaries which he had placed in the library of Trinity College, Cambridge with a time-veto against their possible misuse by would-be biographers, seeking among the memorials of the illustrious dead for evidence of sexual perversities and scandals, rather as little dogs seek out truffles. Some of the happiest summer days of my life were spent among the shelves of that cool and lovely Wren library – with a punt moored on the adjacent Cam in which to eat my sandwich lunch – as I transcribed passages from Macaulay's diaries not used by Sir George Otto Trevelyan in his uncle's classic biography.

Apart from their writings, the lives of writers tend to be uneventful, and, the more they write, the truer this is, since so much of their time has to be spent at their sedentary task. 'Well I suppose it's scribble, scribble,

scribble, Mr Gibbon,' George III remarked to the historian
of the Roman Empire, and there can be few professional
writers who do not feel the force of the royal comment.
Gibbon's fellow historian, Macaulay, is an exception. This
was partly because from his earliest years, growing up in
the heart of the politically orientated Clapham sect, he was
involved in, and, after he reached manhood, actively and
passionately engaged in the great ameliorative and
reforming liberal crusade which, in the latter eighteen-
twenties and early thirties, swept like an incoming tide
over the outdated shibboleths, laws and institutions of
nineteenth-century Britain. His father, Zachary Macaulay,
was the working veteran of the great Evangelical and
humanitarian Movement which, in the course of a lifetime
of struggle, achieved the abolition of the transatlantic slave
trade, and ultimately of slavery itself throughout the
British Empire. Macaulay put into Parliament while still in
his twenties by a great Whig magnate in recognition of the
brilliance of his polemical writings in the liberal cause, was
one of the most eloquent and fiery of all the parliamentary
orators who between 1830 and 1832 broke the long Tory
monopoly of power and, by carrying the Reform Bill on a
great wave of popular indignation and enthusiasm,
brought about an English constitutional revolution without bloodshed or social upheaval. As Gladstone once
said, only Byron and the younger Pitt won fame so
young.

What made Macaulay's success in those dramatic
debates so remarkable was that he had no natural advantages of birth, fortune or even appearance. 'An ugly,
cross-made, splay-footed, shapeless little dumpling,' a
writer in Blackwood's described him, 'with a featureless
face – except, indeed, a good expansive forehead – sleek,
puritanical sandy hair, large glimmering eyes and a mouth

from ear to ear.' A correspondent of the New York *Observer* reported seeing him take the floor in one of the Reform Bill debates : 'a little man, of small voice, affected utterance, clipping his words and hissing like a serpent, "Mr Macaulay", went quickly around among the spectators. The House was still for the first time in the evening, and each fixed his eye upon the little man. . . . And surely I thought them very simple to be attracted by such an unpromising beginning, and utterly perverted in taste to be able even to endure such affected, intolerable elocution. Fortunately however, these spasmodic symptoms gradually wore off as the fire of argument kindled up his soul. . . . In fifteen minutes he had wrapped himself in the Reform Bill as in a mantle and thrown its brilliant and attractive forms over him, . . . and himself stood up, thus invested, challenging and receiving universal admiration.'

In a still intensely aristocratic age and society, without hereditary influence and fortune Macaulay became a junior Minister at thirty-two and, when the Whigs lost office and he had to seek his livelihood outside Westminster, a member of the Supreme Council of India, where he helped to lay the foundations of British policy for the next century. On his return to England, he entered the Cabinet before he was forty as Secretary-at-War, and later, after an interlude of Conservative rule, as Paymaster-General. Widely read as were his popular essays, reviews and ballads, before at the age of 48 he published the still more widely read and acclaimed opening volumes of his great history, he was principally known to his countrymen, not as a mere writer, but as a leading parliamentarian and public figure who had played a yeoman part in the great Reform Bill debates and who, even after he lost his seat at Edinburgh and voluntarily relinquished his Cabinet office in order to devote himself to his history, was re-elected to

Parliament by his former constituents without his having either to canvass or visit them.

That he never reached the highest offices of state was partly due to his uncompromising adherence to the strictest principles of public morality. 'I have always been firmly convinced,' he wrote to one of the newly en-franchised electors of his Leeds constituency at the time of the Reform Bill, 'that the confidence of the English people is to be obtained, not by a sycophancy, which degrades alike those who pay and those who receive it, but by rectitude and plain dealing . . . If ever there was a time when public men were in an especial measure bound to speak the truth, the whole truth and nothing but the truth to the people, this is the time. Nothing is easier than for a candidate to avoid unpopular topics as long as possible, and, when they are forced on him, to take refuge in evasive and unmeaning phrases. Nothing is easier than for him to give extravagant promises while an election is depending, and to forget them as soon as the return is made. I will take no such course. I do not wish to obtain a single vote under false pretences. Under the old system I have never been the flatterer of the great. Under the new system I will not be the flatterer of the people. . . . It is not necessary to my happiness that I should sit in Parliament. It is necessary to my happiness that I should possess, in Parliament or out of Parliament, the consciousness of having done what is right.'

Though an eminently sensible and practical man, and certainly as he grew older no fanatic or prig, throughout his political career Macaulay, utterly incapable of decep-tion, never deviated from this austere resolve. There were two other essentials to his well-being. For all his passionate dedication to, and involvement in the political life of his country, past and present, he was happier in the last resort thinking and writing about it in the calm of his library than debating about its daily course with men of lesser intelligence and perception in the crowded and foetid chambers of the House of Commons. 'I have to sit here from noon to six,' he wrote to a friend during one of his spells on the Treasury Front Bench, 'and, as a great fool is speaking, I might as well write to you as listen to him.' And during his parliamentary exile in India, living at Calcutta in the hot, steamy and near pestilential alluvial swamp of the Ganges delta, he wrote to the same friend, 'I am more comfortable than I expected to be in this country; and as to the climate I think it beyond all comparison better than that of the House of Commons.'

Moreover, as all artists must be – and in his own sphere, the art of recreating the living politics of the past which is history, Macaulay was nothing if not an artist – he was an intensely sensitive and therefore vulnerable man, dependent more than most on the comfort and consolations of private affections to offset the strains and frustrations of public life. With little, or indeed, so far as can be ascertained, any sexual urge at all, his affections were concentrated from an early age on his own family, and, above all, on his two younger sisters, Hannah and Margaret, who, after his father had lost his money, were financially dependent on him. It was for their sake, as much as to secure his own future parliamentary and literary independence, that he undertook, on the threshold of a great parliamentary career, five years of exile from his native land and friends. 'Before I went to India,' he wrote in his journal, 'I had no prospect . . . except that of living by my pen and seeing my sisters governesses.' He might easily, like so many young men of promise in that aristocratic and wealth-orientated age, have married an heiress : the name of one, a pretty society girl with a fortune of £70,000 –

equivalent to at least a million today – was momentarily linked with his in the lobbies. In the year after he entered Parliament, a fellow member wrote, 'I think from what I have seen, that Tom Macaulay will soon have achieved the Kinnaird . . . He must as his next move marry a woman of fortune somehow or other, and, if he does, he is Prime Minister.'

But the reputed bridegroom to be would have none of it. 'My dear, dear girl, my sister – my darling – my own sweet friend – ' he was writing to Hannah a few weeks later, 'you cannot tell how, amidst these tempests of faction and amidst the most splendid circles of our nobles, I pine for your society, for your voice, for your caresses.' And he loved both girls equally, and had done so ever since they were still in the nursery – the one ten and the other twelve years younger than himself. 'There are not ten people in the world whose deaths would spoil my dinner,' he wrote at the time of Wilberforce's death, reflecting on how little the passing of even the greatest friends really affected the daily lives of those who knew them best, 'but there are one or two whose deaths would break my heart.' When a few years later, during his Indian exile, letters from England brought him the news of Margaret's death, he wrote to his lifelong friend, Thomas Flower Ellis, 'What she was to me no words can express. I will not say she was dearer to me than anything in the world, for my sister who is with me was equally dear. But she was as dear to me as one human being can be to another.'

So it was, in this happier period of his life, when he was an ardent young MP living alone in London and his beloved sisters were about to join him there, he wrote gaily as the long parliamentary session drew to a close, 'I am in high spirits at seeing you all in London and of being

again one of a family and of a family which I love so much.'
And when the time came to part, 'Farewell, my dearest
girls. Farewell bird Annie, Nancy, little Anne, farewell
Chilapet. I do not know why it is that all our little jokes
and nicknames come into my head at once and almost make
the tears come into my eyes.' 'My darlings, my loves,' he
told them, 'to you I do not write letters but prattle and
talk nonsense, as we used to do, only that I use my pen
instead of my tongue. Oh, if you knew, my little girls,
what a desert this vast city is without you. How sweet and
perfect a love is that of brothers and sisters.' This intense
playful and deeply emotional devotion to the women of his
family continued all his life; fifteen years later, after his
defeat at Edinburgh, he was writing in the same vein to
Hannah's nine year old daughter, Baba, 'I received your
pretty letter this morning . . . I assure you that I care a
great deal more about you than about my election, and
am far more pleased at having such a dear good little niece
than at being a member of Parliament and a Minister.' And
in the penultimate year of his life, a whole generation
after Margaret's death, he wrote in his journal, 'To think
that she has been near 22 years dead, and I am crying as
if it were yesterday.'

It is these letters to his sisters, relating the events of
his daily life in a vanished age, that help to make
Macaulay's life so fascinating. The immediacy of his de-
scriptive powers equals that of Pepys; his account of the
coronation of William iv in 1831 matches that of the
diarist's picture of Charles ii's coronation a hundred and
seventy-one years before.

My love,
I scarcely know where to begin or where to end my story of
the magnificence of yesterday. No pageant can be conceived
more splendid. I rose at six. The canon awakened me, and as

soon as I got up, I heard the bells pealing on every side from
all the steeples in London. I put on my court-dress and looked a
perfect Lovelace in it. At seven the glass coach which I had
ordered for myself and some of my friends came to the door.
Our party being complete we drove through the crowds of
people and ranks of horse-guards in cuirasses and helmets to
Westminster Hall, which we reached as the clock struck eight.

The House of Commons was crowded. There must have been
four hundred members present, and the aspect of the assembly
was very striking. The great majority were in military or naval
uniforms. All officers in the militia or yeomanry and all the
Deputy-Lieutenants of counties wore their military garb. The
ministers were in their official suits of purple and gold. There
were three or four Highland Chiefs in kilts, plaids and philibegs
with eagles plumes in their hats, dirks and pistols at their sides,
and claymores in their hands. The Speaker came at nine in his
robes of State, covered with gold embroidery. After prayers we
went out in order by lot, the Speaker going last. My county,
Wiltshire, was among the first drawn so I got an excellent
place, next to Lord Mahon, who is a very great favourite of
mine and a very amusing companion, though a bitter Tory.

Our gallery was immediately over the great altar. The whole
vast avenue of lofty arches was directly in front of us. In the
centre of the Abbey, where the nave and transept cross each
other, were several raised steps, covered with a Brussels carpet.
On these steps a footcloth of yellow silk was spread, and the
throne and footstool for the king were in the centre of this cloth.
The Queen's throne was a few steps lower. The Chair in which
the Kings are crowned is different from the Throne. They are
not enthroned till after they have been crowned. The Coronation
Chair I have seen a hundred times. It is one of the shows of the
Abbey, six hundred years old at least; and quite mouldering.
The seat is placed on a stone which Edward the First brought
from Scotland as a trophy. Stone and wood however were now
completely covered with cloth of gold and satin. All the
pavement of the Abbey was covered – with blue cloth and red
cloth in the less conspicuous parts, – with rich carpeting in the

place where the ceremony was to be performed. Vast galleries hung with red cloth were extended between the pillars, and some were hung at a dizzy height far above our heads.

Gradually the body of the Abbey filled with Peers, Peeresses, and Judges, and Bishops, all in full robes, the Peers and Peeresses with coronets in their hands. On our right hand was a gallery filled with the foreign Ambassadors and their ladies. There were Talleyrand, Washington Irving, the Duchess de Dino, the Princess Lieven, and a crowd of others. All the uniforms and orders of Europe might be seen there. Other galleries in our neighborhood were occupied by charming English women, who outbloomed the ladies of the Corps Diplomatique most indisputably.

. . . At eleven the guns fired, the organ struck up, and the procession entered. I never saw so magnificent a scene. All down that immense vista of gloomy arches there was one blaze of scarlet and gold. First came heralds in coats stiff with embroidered Lions, Unicorns and Harps, then nobles dressed in ermine and velvet bearing the Regalia – with pages in rich dresses carrying their coronets on cushions – then the Dean and Prebendaries of Westminster in rich copes of cloth of gold, – then a crowd of beautiful girls and women – or at least of girls and women who at a distance looked altogether very beautiful – attending on the queen. Her train of purple velvet and ermine was borne by six of these fair creatures. All the great officers of state in full robes. The Duke of Wellington with his marshal's staff – the Duke of Devonshire with his white rod, Lord Grey with the Sword of State – and the Chancellor with his seals came in procession. Then all the Royal Dukes with their trains borne behind them, and last the King leaning on two Bishops – I do not,, I dare say, give you the precise order. In fact it was impossible to discern any order. The whole Abbey was one blaze of gorgeous dresses, mingled with lovely necks and faces.

The Queen behaved admirably, with wonderful grace and dignity – the King very ill and awkwardly. The Duke of Devonshire looked as if he came to be crowned instead of his master – I never saw so princely a manner and air. The

Chancellor looked like Mephistopheles behind Margaret in the Church.

The ceremony was much too long, and some parts of it were carelessly performed. The Archbishop mumbled. The Bishop of London preached, well enough indeed, but not so effectively as the occasion required; and, above all, the low, clumsy bearing of the King made the foolish parts of the ritual appear monstrously ridiculous and deprived many of the better parts of their proper effect. Persons who were at a distance perhaps did not feel this. But I was near enough to see every turn of his finger and every glance of his eye. The moment of the crowning was extremely fine. When the Archbishop placed the crown on the head of the King, the trumpets sounded, – the whole audience cried out God save the King. All the Peers and Peeresses put on their coronets, and the blaze of splendour through the Abbey seemed to be doubled.

Or take this account in a lighter vein of the House of Commons going in a body to a royal levee at St James's Palace to address the King on his escape after a discharged Greenwich pensioner had thrown a stone at him and hit his hat :

Oh if you but knew the pleasure of being admitted to the Royal presence! I cannot keep my elation to myself. I cannot describe my feelings in dull creeping prose. I burst forth in unpremeditated verse, worthy of the judicious poet ' – that is himself – ' I so often quote.

> I passed in adorning
> The whole of the morning
>> When the hand of the King must be kissed,
>>> must be kissed.
>
> I put on my back
> A fine suit of black
> And twelve ells of lace on my wrist
>> on my wrist.

I went to the levee
And squeezed through the bevy
Till I made good my way to his fist
                                   to his fist.

But my wing fails me. I must keep in prose for a few lines. At
one we assembled in the House of Commons. For this was the
day appointed for taking up our address to the King. The House
looked like a parterre of tulips – all red and blue .... Much
gold lace was there and much silver lace – many military
uniforms – yeomanry uniforms – navy uniforms, official uniforms ... Then the Speaker rose and walked majestically down
stairs to his state carriage, – an old thing covered with painting
and gilding of the days of Queen Anne. In this huge conveyance
he drove away with the Serjeant at Arms carrying the mace, and
the Chaplain carrying his own fat rotundity – quite load enough,
I assure you. We came behind in about a hundred carriages ...
at hearse pace, forming a string from Westminster Hall to St
James's Palace. The carriage stopped. We alighted at the door
of a long passage, matted, and furnished only with large wooden
benches. Along this passage we went to a stone staircase. On
the landing places guards with their swords and carbines were
in attendance to slay us if we behaved improperly. At the top of
the staircase we passed through two ranks of beef-eaters, blazing
in scarlet and gold, to a table, where we wrote our names, each
on two cards. One card we left on the table with the page. The
other we took with us to give to the Lord in Waiting.

As a member of the House of Commons, I had peculiar
advantages. For before the levee we were admitted to present
our address. The throne room was however so crowded that
while we were going through the ceremony I heard little, and
saw nothing. But I mistake – one thing I saw – a great fool
with a cocked hat and a coat like that of the fifer of a band, Mr
Edwin Pearson, who was performing his duties as Exon. He
condescended to quiz me through his glass, and then to extend
his hand and congratulate me on my appointment. 'Such
instances of elegant breeding,' as Sir William Lucas says, 'are

not uncommon at the Court.' When we had walked out backward, trampling on each other's toes and kicking the skin off each other's shins, the levee began, and we were re-admitted singly to the apartment which we had just left in a body. The King stood near a door. We marched before him and out at a door on the other side, bowing and scraping the whole way. When I came to him, I gave my card to the Lord in Waiting who notified the name to the King. His Majesty put forth his hand. I kneeled, or rather curtseyed, and kissed the sacred object most reverently. Then I walked away backwards bowing down my head like a bulrush, and made my way through the rooms into the street with all expedition.

This is a levee : and a stupid affair it is. I had a thousand times rather have one of the quiet walks which I used to have this time of year with Margery than cuff and kick my way through these fine people – and I would a thousand times rather kiss my Nancy's lips than all the hands of all the kings in heaven.

To the end of his life, as Professor Pinney's superb edition of his *Letters* shows, whenever a foreign holiday or any other temporary cause, separated him from his surviving sister, Hannah – Lady Trevelyan as she became after her marriage – Macaulay continued to draw, for her family's delectation and ours, vivid and enchanting pictures of contemporary life. Witness this account of an old-fashioned French provincial city, Bourges, which he visited on a continental holiday in 1844.

It is the strangest place, an ancient city in the very heart of France, of great historical fame, and in size and population not inferior to Worcester or Ipswich. It was the capital of a great province before the Revolution. It is still the chief town of a departement, and the seat of an Archbishop. And yet one would imagine that the single night which carried me from Paris to Bourges had carried me into a different country, into a country as uncivilised as Lithuania or Servia. Bourges is still the Bourges of Louis the Fourteenth's time. Queer old-fashioned country-gentlemen of long descent who recovered part of their estates on return from emigration abound in the neighbourhood. They have hotels in Bourges where they often pass the winter instead of going up to Paris. Such strange, dingy-looking, antiquated edifices as these hotels I never saw. The shabbiness of the streets is like that of the meaner sort of country towns in Scotland. There is a general air of discomfort and a squalidity which seems to proceed not from poverty, but from want of refinement. There is no lack of courtesy. On the contrary the manners of the people are ceremonious. Hats are off at every word. If you ask your way, a gentlemen insists on escorting you. Did you ever read Georges Dandin? If not read it before you sleep. There you will see how Molière has portrayed the old-fashioned provincial gentry. I could fancy that many Messieurs de Sotenville and Madames de Sotenville would be found at Bourges. I was struck by observing, wretched as is the general look of the place, two coroneted carriages at the doors of private houses. Even at Paris you may walk for an hour in the best quarter of town without seeing a coroneted carriage, unless indeed it be that of an English nobleman.

Or, as he continued his description in a letter to Lady Holland :

These great gentry and the clergy of the Cathedral seem to bear rule in Bourges. The self-importance and the bigotry of the lowest hangers-on of the priesthood surpasses anything that I saw in Flanders. I was at the best inn, and there was no want of courtesy or disposition to oblige. But the discomfort was almost insufferable. The only salon was filled with all the inmates of the house and all the comers and goers of the town, mine host casting up accounts, mine hostess looking over linen, the dogs from the street fighting for a bone, two handmaidens stitching, a little girl learning to write, a little boy learning to read, a coxcomb with a long beard and a cigar in his mouth, an old pantaloon reading a paper three weeks old, a beggar who had poked in his head and a wen larger than his head, at the window, and was whining his 'Pour l'amour de Dieu, Messieurs.'

Lastly there was the Englishman, myself, trying to forget his ill humour in a very naughty but very amusing novel by Paul de Kock.

Yet the man who wrote these charming and playful letters to his sisters was one of the great scholars of his day, with an encyclopaedic mind and an almost miraculous memory stored with ancient and modern learning, and with the prodigous organizational powers which enabled him to write his majestic *History of England* with a clarity and narrative skill never surpassed by any other English historian. During his sojourn in India and his long voyages there and back he read the classics continually, as he did in his leisure moments from politics and his History for the rest of his life. 'I have during this year,' he wrote to Ellis from Calcutta in 1837,

read again all Livy and all Cicero, and I am now going through Tacitus. They are the three great names in the literature of Rome. I put them all decidedly above any of the Latin poets. I have again, in a dawdling way, at odd minutes, gone through Aulus Gellius, who, though a frivolous fellow, is rather a favourite with me. In Greek I have during this year read Homer twice through, the greater part of Plato, Aristotle's Politics, which I think by far his finest work, Thucydides, all Xenophon's works, Philostratus's Life of Appolonius of Tyana, a heap of impudent lies which nevertheless sets one a thinking, some of Nonnus's trash, which tired me to death, Herodian, Polybius, a good many of Plutarch's lives over and over, Lysias twice, a good deal of Isocrates, Longinus, and some of the best speeches of Demosthenes.

And in an earlier letter to him he wrote :

I have ample leisure for literature : and I read with the most ravenous appetite. I mean to go fairly through the whole literature of Greece and Rome before I return. I have often thought that it is sad folly to give the first twenty years of life to the mastering of two such difficult and valuable languages as the Greek and Latin, and then never to open a Greek or Latin book. Scarcely any man of thirty reads much Greek. The consequence is that all our notions about the ancient history, the ancient literature, the ancient modes of society have a certain schoolboy character. They are notions formed before we have seen anything of the world. The ancient writers now that I go back to them at thirty-four, having acquired some knowledge of the literature of France, Italy, Spain and Portugal, having seen something of the world, having been a spectator and an actor in politics, appear quite new to me. I find in such a writer as Thucydides or Demosthenes ten thousand things worthy of notice which never struck me in my college days, which indeed never could possibly strike any young man, however quick and clever. My admiration for the Greeks increases every day. It almost amounts to idolatry. I was a sad heretic about Euripides. I have thoroughly recanted my error, and begin to prefer him to Sophocles. I did not much like Thucydides formerly. I have now no hesitation in pronouncing him the greatest historian that ever lived.

And before he sailed for England he told Ellis that he intended to spend the long voyage round the Cape mastering the literature of Germany.

I intend to make myself a good German scholar by the time of my arrival in England. I have already, at leisure moments, broken the ice. I have read about half of the New Testament in Luther's translation; and am now getting rapidly, for a beginner, through Schiller's History of the Thirty Years' War. At present I can only afford an hour or two in the day for this study. At sea I intend to read German regularly at the rate of ten hours a day. I shall make a complete conquest of the language.

Macaulay was not only a great scholar and a still greater writer; he was, as his letters and journals show, an inherently good man. Honoured at the time of his death above all other writers of the day, and hardly as any other English author has been honoured by his contempories, it was his sister who summed up the essence of the man. 'We have lost the light of our home, the most tender, loving, generous, unselfish, devoted of friends. What he was to me for fifty years how can I tell? What a world of love he poured upon me and mine.' And in the inevitable reaction after his death against the over-certainty of his judgements and the hard metallic clarity of his style, his fellow writer Thackeray saw the real truth of the matter. 'The critic,' he wrote, 'who says that Macaulay had no heart, might say that Johnson had none. Two men more generous, and more loving, and more hating, and more partial, and more noble, do not live in our history.'

1
Youth of a Poet

As to my early bon-mots, my crying for holidays, my walks to school through showers of cats and dogs, I have left all these for the 'Life of the late Right Honourable Thomas Babington Macaulay, with large extracts from his correspondence, in two volumes quarto, by the Very Rev. J. Macaulay, Dean of Durham and Rector of Bishopsgate, with a superb portrait from the picture by Pickersgill in the possession of the Marquess of Lansdowne'!
(Letter by Macaulay to his sisters, Hannah and Margaret, 21 July 1832.)

In the year 1800, when Mr Pitt was Prime Minister and the world was in arms, there was born on St Crispin's Day, in the old Leicestershire manor-house of Rothley Temple, a male child. According to a poem written by the latter half a century later, the fairy queens who pronounce dooms over mortal births were frankly discouraging. The Queen of Gain swept by with careless glance, the Queen of Power frowned, the Queen of Fashion even minced to show her scorn. Only their sister of Poetry bent for a moment over the cradle. But when she rose the babe was seen to be smiling.

Had it been otherwise, the union of a Bristol bookseller's daughter with a prosperous merchant of Scottish descent and Evangelical leanings could scarcely have been blessed with a poet for its first-fruit. They christened him Thomas Babington, after the uncle in whose house he had been born, and took him to London where his father, Zachary Macaulay, was living as secretary of the Sierra Leone

1

Company in Birchin Lane. Here, beneath the shadow of Wren's steeples, Tom Macaulay formed his first impressions of the world. But his true character was not revealed till after his second birthday, when his father, whose life-long passion was a hatred of the slave trade, removed his family to Clapham, then famous as the residence of that little group of friends who had sworn to rid mankind of its greatest curse.

All day Tom would lie before the fire, grasping a piece of bread-and-butter in his hand while he devoured book after book. Everything printed was food to that gigantic appetite – the works of piety which his alarmed parents offered him, vast eighteenth-century novels, above all, poetry. Whatever he read he remembered, weaving its language into his talk. When the grave Hannah More came to call, he invited her to take a glass of old spirits, assuring her that Robinson Crusoe often had some, and when at the age of four he was badly scalded by some spilt coffee, he answered his hostess's inquiries with an heroic 'Thank you, madam, the agony is abated.' We see him in his parents' letters, a frail, fair-haired child, reading Crabbe's *Tales* in the garden, or running, fiercely and impetuously eager, across the hillocks of Mount Sinai and the Clapham Alps, while far away the sails of the English ships crossed and re-crossed the Spanish horizon, and watchers on the Kentish shore caught the distant gleam of Napoleon's waiting bayonets. Yet the background of his life was peaceful enough – the comfortable, unassuming prosperity of his father's household, the drowsy sermons in the parish church, the high-purposed, benevolent families of the Clapham sect from which his playmates were drawn: the Wilberforces, the Grants, the Thorntons, the Stephens.

Soon Tom added the writing of literature to the reading of it. At the age of seven he was at work on a Compendium of Universal History from the Creation to Modern Times, filling a quire of paper and introducing Cromwell as 'a wicked and unjust man', a paper to convert the people of Travancore – where his uncle, Colin Macaulay, was Resident – to Christianity, a poem in six cantos on the Battle of Cheviot in the style of his favourite Walter Scott, an epic on the fortunes of his family, and a number of evangelical hymns. The latter he used to compose at breakfast.

To his mother's old teacher, Hannah More, ever on the lookout for youthful genius, all this was gratifying in the extreme. She delighted to guide the child in his reading, to watch his passionate espousal of the Trojan cause when she read him Pope's *Homer*, to give him volumes with which to form a library of his own – her dear little poet, she called him. Fearing that his busy, eager mind would wear out his frail body, she took him each summer to stay with her at Barley Wood. The house with its roses climbing the trellis, the view of the Mendips, and the islands on the horizon sank into the boy's inner consciousness. He loved to accompany his hostess on her visits through that pleasant countryside, to hear from the garrulous Somerset cottagers tales of Jeffreys' Assize or peer at the chained folio of Foxe's Martyrs in Cheddar Church, to learn to cook in Hannah's kitchen or preach her sermons, standing dramatically on one of the parlour chairs. But most he loved it when at Christmas she gave him *carte blanche* to take his choice of all the Bards of Epic Song displayed in Mr Hatchard's bow-window, to be handsomely bound and adorned with gilt letters and treasured as his very own.

When he was twelve he was sent, dreadfully homesick, to a private school at Little Shelford – soon afterwards removed to Aspenden Park in Hertfordshire. Its master, Preston, was a fine teacher, full of the acute, scholarly spirit of Cambridge, and he soon fired his pupil with his own love for the classics. Gripped by their enchantment the boy became one of the first scholars of that classical age, and so deep was the impression they made on him that he never ceased to survey the problems of his own day from the high places of Athens and Rome.

Deep in Plato and Aristotle, Tom would return for his holidays to fill the house with books and the talk of books. To the grave Zachary this perpetual reading was increasingly disquieting – dram-drinking in the morning, he termed it. Nor did he approve of his eldest son's passionate enthusiasms, his unbrushed hair, and the blots with which he sealed his letters, or the loud and almost unchristian intensity with which he engaged in argument.

From the restraints of his father's home Macaulay passed in 1818 to Cambridge. In the Athenian freedom of Trinity he found himself at liberty to read all day and argue all night, which he generally did, supping in the small hours on roast turkey and milk punch, and ranging all history and philosophy till dawn flushed the grey balustrades and the pale faces of the disputants. Some drawbacks, of course, there were. The ordered curriculum of a university is apt at all times to press on those who are too catholic in their enthusiasms. Macaulay rebelled in particular against Cambridge's favourite study : 'I can scarcely bear', he told his mother, 'to write on Mathematics or Mathematicians. Oh for words to express my abomination of that science! I feel myself becoming a personification of algebra, a living trigonometrical canon, a walking table of logarithms. Farewell, then, Homer, and Sophocles, and Cicero :

"Farewell happy fields,
Where joy for ever reigns! Hail horrors, hail
Infernal world!" '

4

But though his refusal to master these mysteries caused him to fail twice before he graced the Tripos list, in other studies he was brilliantly successful. Twice he gained the Chancellor's Medal for English Verse – a proof, he used to maintain in after years, that his poetry must have been very bad – and in 1821 the Craven Scholarship. And at twenty-three he was awarded the crowning prize of a Cambridge career – a Trinity Fellowship. It meant that for seven years, provided he remained a bachelor, he was sure of £300 a year, a stable for his horse, and six dozen of audit ale every Christmas.

While still at Cambridge, young Macaulay made his first essay in politics.* His father, as befitted the associate of Wilberforce, was a Pittite Tory, and in those austere steps it was expected that Tom should follow. But youth in the hungry, restless years that followed the Napoleonic Wars was turning its back on the old England that had barred herself so stubbornly into her innermost Tory fastness to beat Revolutionary France and remained there ever since. In the debates of the Cambridge Union Society in Petty Cury, the Clapham slave-liberator's son was among the most ardent of those who poured scorn on the hallowed commonplaces of the Tories – a popular but somewhat headlong orator, as a friend's lines attest :

Then the favourite comes, with his trumpets and drums,
And his arms and his metaphors crossed.

To Hannah More, who had regarded her protégé purely as a poet, it was all a little puzzling. And when his parents,

* Within a few weeks of his arrival at the University, he was struck smartly in the face, while standing on the hustings, by a dead cat : an encounter which gave rise, when his assailant explained that he had meant the animal for Mr. Adeane, the Tory candidate, to the rejoinder : 'I wish you had meant it for me and hit Mr Adeane.'

horrified to hear that Tom had been moving in revolutionary society, wrote to protest, they received small comfort. 'Whatever the affectionate alarm of my dear mother may lead her to apprehend,' they were informed, 'I am not one of the sons of anarchy and confusion with whom she classes me. My opinions, good or bad, were learnt, not from Hunt and Waithman, but from Cicero, from Tacitus, and from Milton. They are the opinions which have produced men who have ornamented the world, and redeemed human nature from the degradation of ages of superstition and slavery. I may be wrong as to the facts of what occurred at Manchester [it was the year of Peterloo] but, if they be what I have seen them stated, I can never repent speaking of them with indignation. When I cease to feel the injuries of others warmly, to detest wanton cruelty, and to feel my soul rise against oppression, I shall think myself unworthy to be your son. I could say a great deal more,' he added.

Yet when, before his Cambridge days were over, Macaulay learnt that his father had lost the greater part of his fortune, he accepted the changed circumstances of his life with patience and cheerfulness. He helped to defray the cost of his education by coaching pupils and, as soon as he was able to earn his own livelihood, shouldered the burden of Zachary's debts. In the meantime the easy spacious background of former days had to be abandoned, and the family moved to more cramped quarters in Bloomsbury. Here, in Great Ormond Street, Tom was its life and soul. To his youngest sisters, Hannah and Margaret, these years of financial stringency were, because of him, years of intense happiness. On these two – the Nancy and Meg of his correspondence – he poured out all the wealth of his affection, and they, being clever and sensitive girls, very naturally returned it, regarding their brilliant elder brother with feelings almost of adoration. Every afternoon he would take them for long walks through the City, relating the historical associations of each alley and courtyard or telling them tales, made up during more solitary rambles, of the figures who once haunted them. And all the while between the three there ran the common love of books, whose characters, discussed continually, were more real to them than their living friends. Even bad books formed the subject of this affectionate companionship, and in the evenings, when the day's work was done, Tom would delight his sisters by rattling off from that superb memory of his the descriptions of all the fainting fits in all Kitty Cuthbertson's absurd novels, dwelling with particular relish on that passage which commemorates the excessive sensibility of Lord St Orville :

One of the sweetest smiles that ever animated the face of mortal now diffused itself over the countenance of Lord St. Orville, as he fell at the feet of Julia in a deathlike swoon.

For other loves there was little room. It is strange that in all the closely recorded life of a virile and affectionate man there should be no evidence of a serious love affair. One faint shadow of one there was, and one alone. It is a tradition in the Trevelyan family that once in his youth, spending the summer vacation as he usually did with his Babington cousins at Rothley Temple, Macaulay showed signs of being attracted by a young lady of that family. The two used to disappear every afternoon to a boat on the pond and there, moored beneath the trees, pass the long summer hours in each other's company. Never, so those who remembered him bore witness in after years, did Tom talk so brilliantly or so delightfully as in that far and mellow autumn. Yet even in this enchanted hour the classics, which transmuted every emotion of his life, cast their spell

7

upon him, for the flirtation remained platonic. Nor could it well be otherwise for a young man with no means but a Fellowship, which was provisional on his remaining a bachelor, and with his family growing every year more dependent on him.

To provide for those he loved and carve a career for himself Macaulay turned to the law. The reception given at an anti-slavery meeting to his first public speech seemed to augur an easy avenue to the Woolsack : so much so that Hannah More felt it incumbent on her to write the young advocate 'an humbling letter on the comparative *value* of talents without humility'. It was not unneeded. At his first Mess night on the Northern Circuit he informed an elderly K.C., who had rebuked him for his dangerous practice of retiring for the night with a book and the tallest candle, that he always read in bed at home, and that if he was not afraid of committing parricide and matricide and fratricide, he could hardly be expected to pay much regard to the lives of the bagmen of Leeds. Yet, though his confidence in himself was unbounded, those cautious employers of talent, the Northern attorneys, were slow to recognize his genius. Few briefs came his way. The only forensic triumph he was able to recall in after years was that once at quarter sessions he convicted a boy of stealing a parcel of cocks and hens. Discouraged and lacking the patience to pursue the drudgery of studies which without practical application seemed dry-as-dust, he devoted his time more and more to literature. For Tom Macaulay had another string to his bow.

2

Cocksure Tom

Fine morning. Scene, the great entrance of Holland House.
  Enter Macaulay and Two Footmen in livery.
First Footman.—Sir, may I venture to demand your
    name.
Macaulay.—Macaulay, and thereto I add M.P.
  And that addition, even in these proud halls,
  May well ensure the bearer some respect.
Second Footman.—And art thou come to breakfast with
    our Lord?
Macaulay.—I am: for so his hospitable will,
  And hers—the peerless dame ye serve—hath bade.
First Footman.—Ascend the stair, and thou above shalt
    find,
  On snow-white linen spread, the luscious meal.
            Exit Macaulay upstairs.
(Macaulay to his sister Hannah, 1 June 1831.)

In the year that Macaulay left Cambridge, the most
famous journal in Great Britain was the *Edinburgh Review*.
Founded by Lord Jeffrey and Sydney Smith at the beginning
of the century, it was the champion of the Whig assault
against the Tory Government. Its buff and yellow covers
had enclosed every attack on ancient abuse and vested
privilege for the past quarter century; its readers were all
those who, when the long-awaited Whig victory came,
were to hold power during the next generation. Jeffrey,
still its editor, was always on the lookout for new talent. In
January 1825 he wrote to a friend, 'Can you not lay your
hands on some clever young man who would write for us?'

He had not long to wait. Some contributions to *Knight's Quarterly Magazine* by a group of Cambridge junior graduates gave him his answer, and in the autumn of that year there appeared in the *Edinburgh* the first of Macaulay's historical essays. It was a review of a newly discovered Latin manuscript of Milton's, and took the form of a survey of the poet's life. Full of a fine flamboyance, it had about it something bracing and novel which took the fancy of that jaded post-war generation. All who read it felt the thrill of its quick-marching narrative and the splendour of its purple passages. The youthful Disraeli, travelling south from Abbotsford in the London coach, listened all day to the great publisher Constable bragging of an article in the *Edinburgh*, written, he confided, by a young lawyer of whom he expected great things. 'The more I think,' wrote Jeffrey to its author, 'the less I can conceive where you picked up that style.'

Like Byron after *Childe Harold*, Macaulay awoke one morning to find himself famous. Such of the fashionable world as were both Whig and literary – and in those days there were many – made much of this new lion. He was asked out to dinners and parties, and, a little awkwardly, went. Those who hoped that his appearance would match his romantic style of writing were disappointed. 'Mr. Macaulay,' said one hostess, 'you are so different to what I expected. I thought you were dark and thin, but you are fair and, really, Mr. Macaulay, you are fat.' Yet for all his ungainly build he held himself well, and his face, though frequently disfigured by his impetuous manner of shaving, was pleasantly good-humoured. 'What do I owe you?' he asked on a visit to the barber. 'Oh, sir,' said the latter, 'whatever you usually give the person who shaves you.' 'In that case,' replied Macaulay, 'I should give you a great gash on each cheek.' By far the most striking thing about his society was his conversation. This was both informative and ceaseless. There were some who thought it too ceaseless : 'a book in breeches', observed Sydney Smith, while that polished old gossip of the world, Creevey, set him down for a noisy vulgar fellow. Indeed, there was no getting away from the fact that he was decidedly middle-class – 'an honest good sort of body made out of oatmeal', as Carlyle said, which was scarcely surprising since his father came out of a manse. Yet those who penetrated that over-confident manner generally ended by liking him, for beneath the surface he was essentially lovable.

How lovable only those who saw him in his own home knew. At the house in Great Ormond Street, young Macaulay had two rôles to play – the consoler of his father's irritable and embittered old age and the mainstay of the family finances. Life in that evangelical household was not always easy : on Sundays the old slave liberator, whose proud rigidity was if anything somewhat increased by the consciousness that he owed his keep to others, forbade his children even the relaxation of walking, and regaled them by reading sermons that lasted the whole afternoon and evening. Yet for years Macaulay bore with this meaningless tyranny rather than offend a father who now, like his little sisters, depended on him for bread.

Between his twenty-fifth and thirtieth year, Macaulay gave himself to literature. Then, as he said in after-years, his pen ran like fire. Written for the press, often on circuit and far removed from books, these early essays in the *Edinburgh* redeem their blunders of fact and judgement by their glorious vitality. In 1828 there appeared his first serious historical study, a review of Hallam's *Constitutional History*, in which he unmasked the full partisanship of his attitude towards the seventeenth century. With all the intensity of a living quarrel he struck at the Tories of his

own day through the bodies of the Cavaliers. He had
scarcely time to praise the very Whiggish Hallam – his
'whole spirit is that of the Bench, not of the Bar' – before
he hauled up the flag of his own passionate advocacy.
Strafford was the 'first of the rats', the 'first Englishman to
whom a peerage was a sacrament of infamy', Charles II 'an
effeminate tyrant', his father a murderer, full of 'smiling
rancour' and 'cringing pride', who gave evidence against
his accomplices. Even the latter's death he used as a
scourge for his own living foes, the Tory high-churchmen,
ridiculing 'the royal blood which still cries to Heaven,
every thirtieth of January, for judgements only to be
averted by salt-fish and egg-sauce'. As for the seventeenth-
century Whigs, their very intolerance and injustice in his
inspired sentences became virtues : they were just to the
point of leniency because they merely slew Strafford by their
votes in a Bill of Attainder instead of having him 'torn in
pieces by a mob or stabbed in the back by an assassin'. The
respectable, liberty-loving citizens of nineteenth-century
Britain, having no very strong views of their own about
persons and events so long past and assailed by this
eloquent torrent of love and hatred, accepted those of
Macaulay without question, much as a bewildered jury
submits to the impassioned pleading of a skilful advocate.
Through his young genius the whole focus of English
history became in due course distorted. For one scholar
with sufficient judgement and knowledge of the facts to
correct his superficial generalizations there were a hundred
journalists, schoolmasters and textbook writers ready to
absorb them with uncritical delight and transmit them to
posterity.

Yet history for its own sake was not Macaulay's object
at this period of his life. He had nobler quarry to hunt. In
the essay on Hallam he showed in one telling phrase how

much his thoughts were turning to the political struggles of his own day. They were not unworthy of his attention. For the long period of Tory domination was at last drawing to a close, and before a landscape of widespread national unrest and poverty the embattled Whigs were proclaiming the right of the middle classes to enter the pale of the constitution. 'Already', wrote the young essayist, 'we seem to perceive the signs of unquiet times, the vague presentiment of something great and strange which pervades the community, the restless and turbid hopes of those who have everything to gain, the dimly hinted forebodings of those who have everything to lose.'

For the next two years, therefore, Macaulay's reviews were confined to political questions – to his attack on the doctrinaire Utilitarians and left-wing radicals of his own party, and his more furious onslaught on the Tory idealists, Southey and Sadler. In the former he showed the moderation of his Liberalism : the new world was to be made safe for middling men of reason and property, but the floodgates against popular rule were to be kept closed. 'If they have power,' he wrote of the people, 'they will commit waste of every sort on the estate of mankind and transmit it to posterity impoverished and desolated.' His ideal of self-government was, in fact, strictly limited – based on the abolition of special privileges possessed by one form of property, such as land, over others, the admission of every decent farmer and shopkeeper to the franchise and a pecuniary qualification to exclude the covetous masses. In all this he voiced admirably the educated opinion of his own generation.

In his essay on Southey, Macaulay brought his boisterous common sense to the castigation not of Radical but of Tory theorists. Southey, the conservative Poet Laureate, had published in 1829 some imaginary colloquies on the present state of society between himself and Sir Thomas More, and with these – 'conversations which pass between Mr. Southey and Sir Thomas More, or rather between two Southeys, equally eloquent, equally angry, equally unreasonable, and equally given to talking about what they do not understand' – the young reviewer had a glorious time. Then amid shouts of laughter he got down to the real business of his review, to ridicule poor Southey's dislike of the new industrial system. Macaulay, to whom man's mechanical conquest of nature was a perpetual source of pride, had nothing but scorn for the poet's preference for the old peasant comity of England to the grim and monotonous factory civilization of the new age. 'Here', he mocks, 'is wisdom. Mr. Southey has found out a way in which the effects of manufactures and agriculture may be compared. And what is this way? To stand on a hill, to look at a cottage and a factory and to see which is the prettier!' He was on surer ground when, like the sturdy individualist he was, he attacked Southey for his paternal ideals of government. 'He seems to be fully convinced that it is in the power of government to relieve all the distresses under which the lower orders labour. . . . He conceives that the business of the magistrate is, not merely to see that the persons and property of the people are secure from all attack, but that he ought to be a jack-of-all-trades, architect, engineer, schoolmaster, merchant, theologian, a Lady Bountiful in every parish, a Paul Pry in every house, spying, eavesdropping, relieving, admonishing, spending our money for us and choosing our opinions for us. His principle is, if we understand it rightly, that no man can do anything so well for himself as his rulers, be they who they may, can do it for him, and that a government approaches nearer and nearer to perfection, in proportion as it interferes more and more with the habits and notions of individuals.'

Macaulay's championship gave to the Whigs, encompassed as they were both by the ancient hostility of the Tories and the envying distrust of their Radical allies, a last triumphant lease of life. To a cause which a long spell of wealth had rendered stale and uninspiring he lent vitality and militant force. His advocacy – popular because never for a moment was it out of touch with the instinctive prejudices of the English middle classes – gave to that dying aristocratic party (with whose historic traditions he had fallen in love) a power and a popularity out of all proportion to its size and aims. Thanks largely to his pen and to the personality of one who had much in common with him, Palmerston, the Whig cause flourished for a further generation with a lustre it had scarcely known in the days of its zenith. When these two died, English Whiggery died also.

Before he was thirty, though he was not in Parliament and was by birth outside the Whig pale, Macaulay's force as a politician was beginning to be recognized. By a curious irony the first official tribute to his genius came from a Tory Chancellor, Lord Lyndhurst, a Trinity man like himself, who in 1829 made him a Commissioner of Bankruptcy. The post brought him £400 a year and a few nominal duties whose nature he described in one of his delightful letters to Hannah :

So here I am, with three of the ugliest attorneys that ever deserved to be transported sitting opposite to me; a disconsolate-looking bankrupt, his hands in his empty pockets, standing behind; a lady scolding for her money and refusing to be comforted because it is not; and a surly butcher-like looking creditor, growling like a house-dog, and saying as plain as looks can say : 'If I sign your certificate, blow me, that's all!' Among

15

these fair and interesting forms, on a piece of official paper, with a pen and with ink found at the expense of the public, am I writing to my Darling.

His new emolument – with his Fellowship and the earnings of his pen it brought his income to about £900 a year – opened to Macaulay the gateway to a great career. In February 1830, while staying with the Wilberforces at Highwood Hill, he received a letter from the Whig magnate, Lord Lansdowne, offering him the pocket-borough of Calne. Speechless with excitement Macaulay flew into Wilberforce's study and put the letter into his hands; a second afterwards he was startled by the old statesman's cry of delight as he recalled his own parliamentary triumphs: 'Ah, I hear that shout again: *"Hear! Hear!"* What a life it was!' A week later, he was staying in the comfortable splendour of Bowood, nourishing himself on 'oceans of beer and mountains of potatoes', and making a leisurely canvass of his respectful constituents.

Macaulay entered the House of Commons at the very end of the long era of Whig exclusion. On 5 April 1830 he made his maiden speech. Three months later George IV and the Tory monopoly went out together. When the new Parliament met in October – the member for Calne, after an automatic re-election, had spent the recess in Paris writing a book on the historical lessons of that summer's bourgeois revolution – the Tory majority had crumbled to nothing. On 13 November the Ministry was defeated, and for the first time in almost fifty years the Whigs were in.

On 1 March 1831 Macaulay was in his place as the curtain went up on the last of the great dramas of the old House of Commons, when Lord John Russell rose to introduce the Reform Bill. Next night, speaking on behalf of the measure, he established his reputation as a parliamentarian. His speech was set off by no oratorical graces; his action was clumsy and his voice harsh and loud. But what he said was packed with telling fact and illustration, of which his wonderful memory ensured that not one line or shade was lost. And his sincerity – the quality which above all others wins the respect of the House – was obvious. The vehemence of his thoughts was transmitted to his speech as he made his final and passionate appeal to his fellow members to pass the Bill before it was too late :

Turn where we may, within, around, the voice of great events is proclaiming to us, Reform, that you may preserve. Now, therefore, while everything at home and abroad forebodes ruin to those who persist in a hopeless struggle against the spirit of the age, now, while the crash of the proudest throne of the Continent is still resounding in our ears, now, while the roof of a British palace affords an ignominious shelter to the exiled heir of forty kings, now, while we see on every side ancient institutions subverted and great societies dissolved, now, while the heart of England is still sound, now, while old feelings and old associations retain a power and a charm which may too soon pass away, now, in this your accepted time, now, in this your day of salvation, take counsel, not of prejudice, not of party spirit, not of the ignominious pride of a fatal consistency, but of history, of reason, of the ages which are past, of the signs of this most portentous time. Pronounce in a manner worthy of the expectation with which this great debate has been anticipated, and of the long remembrance which it will leave behind. Renew the youth of the state. Save property, divided against itself. Save the multitude, endangered by its own ungovernable passions. Save the aristocracy, endangered by its own unpopular power. Save the greatest and fairest and most highly civilised community that ever existed from calamities which may in a few days sweep away all the rich heritage of so many ages of wisdom and glory. The danger is terrible. The time is short. If this Bill should be rejected, I pray to God that none of those who concur in rejecting it may ever remember their votes with unavailing remorse, amidst the wreck of laws, the confusion of ranks, the spoliation of property, and the dissolution of social order.

'Portions of that speech', said the leader of his foes, Sir Robert Peel, 'were as beautiful as anything I ever heard or read. It reminded me of the old times.'

There followed for Macaulay three years of eager political life, with the future leadership of the triumphant Whigs and the premiership as the glittering prizes before him. In these years he appears as a true House of Commons man, entering with ardent enthusiasm into the life of what was then the best club in the world, attending every debate and division and walking home at midnight for a supper of cheese and beer in his chambers in Gray's Inn. He was the strongest and most whole-hearted of partisans. 'You might have heard a pin drop', he wrote on the night the Reform Bill passed its second reading by one vote, 'as Duncannon read the numbers. Then again the shouts broke out, and many of us shed tears. I could scarcely refrain. And the jaw of Peel fell; and the face of Twiss was as the face of a damned soul; and Herries [they were all Tories] looked like Judas taking his neckcloth off for the last operation. We shook hands, and clapped each other on the back, and went out laughing and crying and huzzaing into the lobby.' And when his chiefs seemed to weaken and spoke of resignation Macaulay, like all good Government back-benchers, was eager with his friends to form a new administration. In that busy existence, with its daily contacts with a hundred personalities, his judgement and knowledge of men steadily widened. It was a life admirably suited to the training of a future historian of a parliamentary nation.

Political reputation brought to Macaulay social success of a kind never won in England by mere literature. The doors of the holy of holies of high Whig society opened at the magic of his speeches; and for a time that stocky middle-class figure graced every gathering of the closest and most aristocratic society this country has ever seen. As long as it was new to him he entered into it with his usual zest, talking volubly all the time, while he dined in state at Lord Grey's, or breakfasted with the wits at Samuel Rogers', or listened in vast gilt salons to 'flute-playing by the first flute-player in England, and pianoforte-strumming by the first pianoforte-strummer in England, and Signor Rubini's incomparable tenor and Signor Curioni's incomparable counter-tenor'. In such society he met everybody – politicians, wits, distinguished foreigners like Talleyrand, even a lady novelist, whom he encountered, as he put it, face to face, lion to lioness. And one day at Lansdowne House, as he was squeezing his way through the crowd beside Sir James Macdonald, he heard a commanding voice saying, 'Sir James, introduce me to Mr. Macaulay,' and there stood a large, bold-looking woman with the remains of a fine person and the air of Queen Elizabeth. 'Macaulay,' said Sir James, 'let me present you to Lady Holland.' Before he knew where he was, he was accepting an invitation to dine and sleep at Holland House.

All this Macaulay transmitted to his little sisters. When he was not free to take his morning walk with them through the Bloomsbury squares, talking of book, or metaphysics or the manuscript of his latest essay, he would write them long amusing letters describing his doings – the new court-dress in which he 'looked a perfect Lovelace, or the Jewish banker's *bal costumé* which he and his brother Charles attended :

I set off a little after ten, having attired myself simply as for a dinner party. The house is a very fine one. The door was guarded by peace-officers, and besieged by starers. . . . Old Goldsmid met me in a superb court-dress, with his sword at his side. . . . There was a most sumptuous-looking Persian, covered with gold lace. Then there was an Italian bravo with a long beard. Two old gentlemen, who ought to have been wiser, were fools enough to come in splendid Turkish costumes at which everybody laughed. . . .

You must not suppose that the company was made up of these mummers. There was Dr. Lardner, and Long, the Greek Professor in the London University, and Sheil, and Strutt, and Romilly, and Owen the philanthropist. Owen laid hold on Sheil and gave him a lecture on Co-operation which lasted for half-an-hour. At last Sheil made his escape. Then Owen seized Mrs. Sheil, – a good Catholic and a very agreeable woman, – and began to prove to her that there could be no such thing as moral responsibility. I had fled at the first sound of his discourse, and was talking with Strutt and Romilly, when behold! I saw Owen leave Mrs. Sheil and come towards us. So I cried out 'Sauve qui peut!' and we ran off. But before we had got five feet from where we were standing, who should meet us face to face but old Basil Montague! 'Nay, then,' said I, 'the game is up. The Prussians are on our rear. If we are to be bored to death there is no help for it.' Basil seized Romilly; Owen took possession of Strutt; and I was blessing myself on my escape, when the only human being worthy to make a third with such a pair, William Smith, caught me by the arm, and begged to have a quarter of an hour's conversation with me. While I was suffering under William Smith a smart impudent looking young dog, dressed like a sailor in a blue jacket and check shirt, marched up, and asked a Jewish looking damsel near me to dance with him. I thought that I had seen the fellow before; and, after a little looking, I perceived that it was Charles; and most knowingly, I assure you, did he perform a quadrille with Miss Hilpah Manasses.

If I were to tell you all that I saw I should exceed my ounce. There was Martin the painter, and Procter, alias Barry Cornwall, the poet or poetaster. . . . I did not see one Peer, or one star, except a foreign order or two, which I generally consider as an intimation to look to my pockets. A German knight is a dangerous neighbour in a crowd. . . . After seeing a gallopade very prettily danced by the Israelitish women, I went downstairs, reclaimed my hat, and walked into the dining-room. There with some difficulty I squeezed myself between a Turk and a Bernese peasant, and obtained an ice, a macaroon, and a glass of wine. Charles was there, very active in his attendance on his fair Hilpah. I bade him good night. 'What!' said young Hopeful, 'are you going yet?' It was near one o'clock; but this joyous tar seemed to think it impossible that anybody could dream of leaving such delightful enjoyments till daybreak. I left him staying Hilpah with flagons, and walked quietly home. But it was some time before I could get to sleep. The sound of fiddles was in mine ears : and gaudy dresses, and black hair, and Jewish noses, were fluctuating up and down before mine eyes. There is a fancy ball for you. If Charles writes a history of it, tell me which of us does it best.

Through the pageant of politics and society Macaulay moved, the same simple unaffected fellow he had always been. The state of his finances was causing him consider-able anxiety – so much so that he was forced to sell the gold medals he had won at Cambridge – for the family was becoming increasingly dependent on him, and the expiry of his Fellowship in 1831 would leave him with no other income than what his pen and his salary as a Bankruptcy Commissioner brought him. Even the latter soon ceased, for the reforming activities of his party reformed away his own superfluous office. It also deprived him of his seat, which was among the pocket-boroughs disfranchised by the Reform Bill.

This loss was instantly made good by Macaulay's re-election by the new middle-class constituency of Leeds. Electioneering under the changed conditions was a little more strenuous – speaking and hearing other people speak as he told his sister, squeezing and being squeezed, shaking hands with people he had never seen before and whose faces and names he forgot within a minute after being introduced to them. 'They feed me', he wrote, 'on roast beef and Yorkshire pudding . . . at night they put me into capital bedrooms and the only plague which they give me is that they are always begging me to mention some food or wine for which I have a fancy.' Such a respectable, industrious, middle-class constituency – there were no more than four thousand electors in all – suited Macaulay's tastes admirably.

The young member's growing party zeal and his readiness to defend the Government in every debate won its reward. In the summer of 1832 he was appointed a Commissioner of the Board of Control, the official body which enforced the will of the British Government on the directors of the East India Company, and before the end of the year he succeeded his old Cambridge friend, Villiers, as its Secretary. For the next eighteen months he led the life of a junior Minister, spending the mornings in his office, 'deep in Zemindars, Ryots, Polygars, Courts of Phousdary, and Courts of Nizamut Adawlut', and his evenings in the apoplectic atmosphere of the old hall of St Stephen's, replying to questions, snubbing the Opposition, and shuffling at the call of the Whips through the Lobbies.

We gained a victory last night [he told his sister in rhyme]
    as great as e'er was known.
We beat the Opposition upon the Russian loan.
They hoped for a majority, and also for our places.

We won the day by seventy-nine. You should have seen
    their faces!
Old Croker, when we shouted, looked heavenly blue with
    rage.
You'd have said he had the cholera in the spasmodic stage.
Dawson was red with ire as if his face was smeared with
    berries;
But of all human visages the worst was that of Herries.
Though not his friend, my tender heart I own could not but
    feel
A little for the misery of poor Sir Robert Peel.
But hang the dirty Tories! and let them starve and pine!
Huzza for the majority of glorious seventy-nine!

In such ding-dong tussling, the eternal lot of party
politicians, the human judgement is apt to become a little
hysterical. Sometimes when the Government was threatened
it seemed to Macaulay that there was nothing before the
country but disaster – a frantic conflict between extreme
opinions, a short period of oppression, a convulsive reaction, and then a tremendous crash of Funds, Church,
Peerage, and Throne. At other times his sense of historical
proportion re-asserted itself; then he would tell his sister :
'To the historian three centuries hence this letter will be
invaluable. To you, ungrateful as you are, it will seem
worthless.' Happily there was always time to write to his
little confidantes, quizzing them in the manner of Swift to
Stella :

        Be you Foxes, be you Pitts,
        You must write to silly chits.

There was also time, astonishingly enough, for literature.
The long succession of reviews for the *Edinburgh* continued – Hampden's, Byron's, and Burleigh's Lives, joyful
attacks on his foes, Montgomery the poetaster, and

Croker the high Tory hack; and an article on the *Pilgrim's Progress*, so popular that an old gentleman in the Athenæum was heard to ask the waiter if the book was in the library. More and more he was bearing the weight of the *Edinburgh* – whose editorship he had recently declined in favour of his friend Macvey Napier – on his shoulders. His work was steadily improving in quality: in 1833 he wrote two articles in a new and more mature vein – the review of Horace Walpole's *Letters* and the first essay on Chatham. And in the same year there appeared, in an anthology of mawkish verse, a ballad that opened like a trumpet call:

> Attend, all ye who list, to hear our noble England's
>   praise.
> I tell of the thrice famous deeds she wrought in ancient
>   days,
> When that great fleet invincible against her bore in vain
> The richest spoils of Mexico, the stoutest hearts of Spain;

and told in galloping heptametres the story of England's homeric age:

> With his white hair unbonneted, the stout old sheriff
>   comes;
> Behind him march the halberdiers; before him sound
>   the drums;
> His yeomen round the market cross make clear an ample
>   space;
> For there behoves him to set up the standard of Her
>   Grace;

and of the pulse of a great people quickening to arms:

> Night sank upon the dusky beach, and on the purple sea,
> Such night in England ne'er had been nor e'er again
>   shall be.

It was an heroic effort for a junior Minister.

He was not without heroism in other things that year. In July he was helping to pilot through the House the new India Bill, transferring the property of the East India Company to the trustees of the Crown, when a measure of a different sort put all his courage to the test. The Ministry of which he was a member had made itself responsible for the emancipation of the West Indian slaves, and a Bill for that purpose was brought before Parliament. But in order to make the change as little hurtful as possible to the planters the final act of emancipation was to be delayed for a term of years. To old Zachary such a proposal seemed the counsel of the prince of darkness : he had given his all for the slaves, and he wished, before he died, to see them free. His son, who had no strong feelings on the matter and certainly had no wish to be a martyr, immediately laid his career and his ambitions on the altar of his father's principles. He informed his chiefs that he must speak and vote against the measure, and according to constitutional practice placed his resignation in their hands. Nor could the arguments of any of his friends move him from this course.

On 24 July he spoke against the Bill. Two days later he learnt that the Cabinet had decided not to accept his resignation and to reduce the delaying term of compulsory 'apprenticeship' for negro slaves from twelve to seven years. The concession satisfied Zachary and saved his son's career.

Yet Macaulay's position was still uncertain and perplexing. Without a private income, as he said, it was not easy for a public man to be honest and almost impossible for him to be thought so. Filled with honourable ambition and loving the work of his office, he knew that the defeat of the Ministry must mean the end of his hopes. The loss of an official salary, a mere bagatelle to his richer colleagues, would leave him no means of support for himself and his family but his pen. And he knew that a literary livelihood and a parliamentary career were incompatible.

When, therefore, his colleagues, who appreciated his situation, made him a tentative offer of a seat on the new Supreme Council of India, Macaulay could not afford to disregard it. The post, if he accepted it, would mean long exile from all that he loved – his home, the intellectual society of London, the excitement and good-fellowship of the House of Commons. On the other hand, it would bring him a salary of £10,000 a year, of which, after supplying the needs of his family and meeting all outgoings on his official position, he would be able to save at least half, and so return to England at the end of six or seven years what he longed to be – a man of independent means. In this crisis one consideration above all others swayed him. A year before his sister Margaret had, to his intense grief, married, and of the two beings to whom he had so unreservedly given his heart only one remained to him. To her he now wrote, begging her to do the one thing which could render the loneliness of exile bearable. 'I can bribe you', he added, 'only by telling you that, if you will go with me, I will love you better than I love you now, if I can.' So entreated, Hannah agreed. Macaulay hesitated no longer. In October the Government was informed of his readiness to accept the post, and before November was over he was writing in triumph that he was about to dine with the Directors of the East India Company, 'now my servants, next week I hope to be my masters'.

3

Indian Administrator

If it be asked whether or not the Penal Code fulfils
the ends for which it was framed, the answer may safely
be left to the gratitude of Indian Civilians, the younger
of whom carry it about in their saddle-bags, and the
older in their heads.
(Sir G. O. Trevelyan, *Life of Macaulay*.)

On 15 February 1834, Macaulay sailed from Gravesend in
the *Asia*. Everybody had been kindness itself, overwhelming him with farewell invitations and affectionate advice.
Even Bobus Smith, Sydney's brother, had added his quota,
urging him to take care always to have at his table some
fleshy, blooming young writer or cadet, just come out, so
that the mosquitoes would stick to him and leave the rest
of the company alone. The traveller took with him –
besides his sister and her maid – his old clerk (he did not
need him but could not bear to throw him out of work) and
a vast number of books. So equipped, he passed southwards
towards the sun, watching the changing stars a little sadly
and reading incessantly, while Hannah on deck read with
the ladies and chatted with the gentlemen. Deep in his
cabin he devoured his books – Greek, Latin, Spanish,
French, and English; folios, quartos, octavos, and duo-
decimos. 'I read insatiably,' he wrote to his old friend
Ellis, 'the *Iliad* and *Odyssey*, Virgil, Horace, Caesar's
Commentaries, Bacon's *de Augmentis*, Dante, Petrarch,
Ariosto, Tasso, *Don Quixote*, Gibbon's *Rome*, Mill's *India*,
all the seventy volumes of Voltaire, Sismondi's *History of*

France, and the seven thick folios of the *Biographia Britannica.'*

After sixteen weeks of voyaging the exiles saw the peaks of the mountains of Ceylon, and on 10 June came to anchor off Madras. Here Macaulay received a summons to join Lord William Bentinck, the Governor-General, at Ootacamund in the hills beyond Mysore. Leaving Hannah to continue the voyage to Calcutta, he set foot on alien and mysterious land. It was all indescribably strange, travelling in a palanquin with thirty-eight attendants into country ever more unfamiliar, amid 'dark faces with white turbans and flowing robes, the trees not our trees, the very smell of the atmosphere that of a hothouse, and the architecture as strange as the vegetation'. He passed through Arcot, the scene of Clive's defence, riding – a somewhat rare feat for him – through the mango garden and Seringapatam, where his historic imagination again took fire at the exploits of his countrymen. Here in the Residency he encountered an immortal fool, an English divine who (as he wrote to Ellis), without any preface, accosted him thus : 'Pray, Mr. Macaulay, do not you think that Buonaparte was the Beast?' 'No, sir, I cannot say that I do.' 'Sir, he was the Beast. I can prove it. I have found the number 666 in his name. Why, Sir, if he was not the Beast, who was?' This was a puzzling question, and I am not a little vain of my answer. 'Sir,' said I, 'the House of Commons is the Beast. There are 658 members of the House; and these, with their chief officers – the three clerks, the Serjeant and his deputy, the Chaplain, the door-keeper, and the librarian – make 666.' 'Well, Sir, that is strange. But I can assure you that, if you write Napoleon Buonaparte in Arabic, leaving out only two letters, it will give 666.'

'And pray, Sir, what right have you to leave out two

letters? And, as St. John was writing Greek, and to
Greeks, is it not likely that he would use the Greek rather
than the Arabic notation?' 'But, Sir,' said this learned
divine, 'everybody knows that the Greek letters were never
used to mark numbers.' I answered with the meekest look
and voice possible: 'I do not think that everybody knows
that. Indeed I have reason to believe that a different
opinion – erroneous no doubt – is universally embraced by
all the small minority who happen to know any Greek.' So
ended the controversy. The man looked at me as if he
thought me a very wicked fellow; and, I dare say, has by
this time discovered that, if you write my name in Tamul,
leaving out T in Thomas, B in Babington, and M in
Macaulay, it will give the number of this unfortunate
Beast.' Refreshed by this interview, Macaulay passed over
the Neilgherries to Ootacamund.

Here he remained till September, enjoying the hospitality
of the most courteous of Governor-Generals and delighting
that unassuming gentleman with his inexhaustible information. To that store he was now adding fast. When the
monsoon was over he resumed his journey to Calcutta,
noting for his letters to Ellis every feature of the Indian
scene about him. The colour and beauty of it touched
springs of poetry never far beneath the surface :

After going down for about half an hour we emerged from
the cloud and moisture, . . . and the immense plain of Mysore
lay before us, – a vast ocean of foliage on which the sun was
shining gloriously. I am very little given to cant about the
beauties of nature, but I was moved almost to tears. I jumped
out of the palanquin, and walked in front of it down the immense
declivity. In about two hours we descended about three thousand
feet. . . . Every turning of the road showed the boundless forest
below in some new point of view. I was greatly struck with the
resemblance which this prodigious jungle, as old as the world,

29

and planted by nature, bears to the fine work of the great English landscape gardeners. It was exactly a Wentworth Park. . . . as large as Devonshire. . . . I was for several hours passing through a succession of scenes which might have been part of the Garden of Eden. Such gigantic trees I never saw. In a quarter of an hour I passed hundreds, the smallest of which would bear a comparison with any of those oaks which are shown as prodigious in England. The grass, the weeds, and the wild flowers grew as high as my head. The sun, almost a stranger to me, was now shining brightly. When in the afternoon I got out of my palanquin and looked back, I saw the huge mountain ridge from which I had descended about twenty miles behind me, still buried in the same mass of fog and rain in which I had been living for weeks.

By November the new Member of the Supreme Council, whose coming had been so much canvassed in Anglo-Indian Society, had set up his establishment, with his sister to preside over it, in a stately Calcutta mansion. Within little more than a fortnight of his doing so all seemed in the dust. Among his earliest callers was a young civilian named Trevelyan, with whom his work brought him into frequent contact. It soon became obvious that Trevelyan had fallen desperately in love with Hannah. The young lady's first reaction was one of distaste: for her wooer, after long exile in a remote part of India, was decidedly awkward, his sole topics of conversation even in courtship being navigation, the education of the natives, the equalization of the sugar duties, and the substitution of the Roman for the Arabic alphabet in Oriental languages. But after a few days Macaulay noticed that his sister was listening to his caller's political disquisitions with more interest. Next day he missed some official papers, and found that Hannah had stolen them and was poring over some powerful but rather too vehement minutes which

Trevelyan had written. Then she began to talk about the Oriental alphabet. Then she engaged a native to teach her Hindustani. Her eyes looked bright when she met Trevelyan on the racecourse, and her cheeks turned extremely red when he spoke to her. In short, as poor Macaulay saw, she became as much in love with him as he was with her.

It would have been easy enough for Macaulay to have stopped the affair, for he knew that the young man's pride was so sensitive that the smallest rebuff would have discouraged him. But he also knew that, however great his own suffering might be, he had no right to enjoy his sister's society at the expense of her happiness. 'Whatever prudes may chuse to say,' he wrote, 'nature made the two sexes for each other. It is the fundamental law on which the whole universe rests that they should mutually attract each other. The celibacy of women has always been to me an object of more pity than I can express.' Macaulay would as soon have locked his beloved Nancy in a nunnery as put the smallest obstacle in the way of her having a good husband. Therefore he gave the lovers his blessing.

Fortunately the kind gods who watched over his life could scarcely have contrived a more eligible brother-in-law. Charles Trevelyan, the most promising young Civilian in the service, was all that he loved a man to be – industrious, honest and courageous, possessed of the highest liberal principles and filled with a passion for progress. His early education having been somewhat neglected, this paragon regarded Macaulay, who was never happier than when employing his natural gift for teaching, with feelings approaching veneration, and hung on his every word. He gladly fell in with his bride's suggestion that they should set up house with her brother, and proposed to postpone his furlough home, which was due, until the time of Macaulay's own return to England.

Yet, though freed from the horror of an immediate separation, Macaulay's heart was sore enough. He had given it many years before without reservation to his two little sisters. For their sake he had put aside all thought of marrying, and the sacrifice had endeared them to him the more. Yet the slightest forethought must have warned him that the very qualities which made them so dear to him would probably make them equally dear to others. He had staked his happiness without calculating the chances of the dice. Two years before Margaret had left home to marry; since then he had lavished all his devotion on Hannah. Now she had gone also. The first place in her affection was given to another, and from now on every year must see some new object of love arise to depress him lower and lower in the scale of her regard till he became no more to her than his own uncles and aunts had been to his father and mother. It was the fundamental law of all society that it should be so.

All this Macaulay hid from Hannah. But to one person he had to own it. In a long and passionate letter he poured out his grief and loneliness to Margaret. 'I have known exile, but I never knew unhappiness before,' he wrote. 'So here you have my heart in all its inconsistency and weakness.' But Margaret never knew of his grief, for fate had one more blow in store for him. When the letter reached England, she was in her grave.

For such a man as Macaulay work is the most sure solvent for grief. And work, and of a kind he loved, there was ample for him. To the task of liberalizing the administration of the conservative East, he now bent all his vast talents and energies. At the time of his coming, India was at the turning of the ways. For good or evil England had constituted herself her moral preceptor. Was the future education of India to proceed on traditional lines, or was it to turn from the Orient and the past to embrace the culture and political idealism of the West? The ten English gentlemen who constituted the Committee of Public Instruction for Bengal were equally, and somewhat warmly, divided in this controversy. Macaulay's appointment as President of the Committee turned the scale. On 2 February he laid before the Supreme Council of India a Minute embodying his views and announcing his intention of resigning if they were not accepted. Were we, he asked scornfully of the advocates of oriental learning, when by teaching English we could advance sound philosophy and true history, to countenance at the public expense 'medical doctrines which would disgrace an English farrier, astronomy which would move laughter in the girls at an English boarding school, history abounding with kings thirty feet high and reigns thirty thousand years long, and geography made up of seas of treacle and seas of butter?' To Macaulay all the learning of the East was nothing beside the metaphysics of Locke and the physics of Newton – a little hocus-pocus about the uses of cusa-grass and the modes of absorption into the Deity. Our business, he held, must be to teach English – the key 'to all the vast intellectual wealth which all the wisest nations of the world have created and hoarded in the course of ninety generations'. So, he argued, a great impulse would be given to the mind of a whole society, prejudices would be overthrown, knowledge diffused, taste purified, arts and sciences planted in lands hitherto barbarous : 'We must do our best to form a class who may be interpreters between us and the millions whom we govern – a class of persons, Indian in blood and colour, but English in taste, in opinions, in morals, and in intellect.' Probably no more momentous Minute has ever been penned. Macaulay's arguments seemed unanswerable. On 7 March 1835 the Governor-General decided that the British Government was under a moral obligation to promote European literature and science among the natives of India. As Sir George Trevelyan, writing in 1876, hopefully put it, the regeneration of our Eastern Empire had begun. Reaping the harvest that the enlightened and reforming spirits of those days sowed, we are perhaps less certain.

Macaulay at once embarked on his duties as President of the Committee responsible for putting these principles into being. For all practical purposes he was the first Director of European Education for India, and at a time when not the most elementary machinery for such education existed. Only about £3,000 a year was at his disposal for the regeneration of two hundred and fifty million people. Yet it was not in his nature to be turned back from any task he had set himself. He saw his goal clearly before him. Competitive examination, ability on the part of every aspirant to office to read, write and work a sum, liberal views on the history of parliamentary assemblages at Westminster, and the correct spelling of English words were henceforward to be the open-sesame to advancement in the land, as Macaulay wrote in his essay on Warren Hastings, of 'the rice-field, the tank, the huge trees, older than the Mogul Empire, under which the village crowds assemble, the thatched roof of the peasant's hut, the rich tracery of the mosque where the *imaum* prays with his face to Mecca, the drums and banners and gaudy idols, the devotee swinging in the air, the graceful maiden with the pitcher on her head descending the steps to the river-side, the black faces, the long beards, the yellow streaks of sect, the turbans and the flowing robes, the spears and the silver maces'. Before long over a thousand Hindu boys at Hooghly College were learning English. The effect of this, as Macaulay wrote to his father, must surely be prodigious : no Hindu boy who received an English education could ever remain sincerely attached to his own religion, and, if his plans of education were followed up, in thirty years' time there would not be a single idolater left among the respectable classes in Bengal. 'I heartily rejoice in the prospect,' he added.

Yet, despite his indignation at anything that offended against the canons of Whig enlightenment – such as Mr Sutherland's enthusiasm for Oriental literature or the 'lion rampant, with a folio in his paw, a telescope over his head, and a Persian motto under his feet' with which the Heralds' College proposed to dignify Hooghly College – the President of the Committee of Public Instruction never failed to appreciate homely commonsense when he met it. When his brother-in-law, shocked by the corrupting influence of the Zenana, proposed to remove the young recipients of Western culture from their incorrigibly Eastern mothers, Macaulay replied that he would prefer a boy of three to lisp all the bad words in the language than to have no feeling of family affection. And when the pedants of his staff proposed to supply their charges with Dick's *Moral Improvement*, Young's *Intellectual Philosophy*, and Chalmers' *Poetical Economy*, they were informed by their Chief that he would rather order a hundred copies of *Jack the Giant-Killer* for his schools than all the grammars of rhetoric or logic ever written.

In fact Macaulay was far too shrewd to be blinded by India as she was : only his boundless faith in the future misled him here, as in other things. He saw clearly enough the existing limitations of the Indian people – 'A race', he wrote, 'so accustomed to be trampled on by the strong that they always consider humanity as a sign of weakness.' If his too sanguine hopes were responsible for something perilous in the British rule of India, his sound sense contributed to much that was wisest in it. 'India cannot have a free government,' he wrote in one Memorial; 'but she may have the next best thing, a firm and impartial despotism.'

That contribution, his first service to India, he began to make soon after his arrival in the East. The Act of 1833, which he had helped to pilot through the House of Commons, provided for the appointment of a Commission to inquire into the Jurisdiction of British India. Macaulay became its first President. The idle apprentice of Lincoln's Inn and the Northern Circuit threw himself into his task with astonishing enthusiasm. The Indian Criminal Code was the fruit of three years' unstinted labour. Others, with greater legal knowledge and wider experience of India, bore much of the heat and dust of the day, but the inspiring genius of the Code was Macaulay's alone. Framed, as he put it, on two great principles – that of suppressing crime with the smallest possible amount of suffering and that of ascertaining truth at the smallest possible cost of time and money – it was written in a style concise and even beautiful. There was no legal pedantry about it: the very wigs of the Judges in the Court of King's Bench would stand on end, its author told Ellis, if they knew how short his chapter on evidence was to be. Like Johnson's *Dictionary*, it abounded in homely and telling illustrations, such as could be trusted to remain in the memory of a busy magistrate. As was natural it was subjected by the Anglo-Indian legal profession to every sort of narrow criticism and obstruction, and its author slandered and vilified. Though completed in 1837, it was not put into operation until 1862. It became an essential part of the heritage of British India.

The three and a half years of Macaulay's stay in the

East were of immense value to him. They taught him the art of administration and – what is of greater importance to an historian – its difficulties. To the surprise of those who knew him he displayed in his work a patience and a readiness to listen to and conciliate the opinions of others which they had believed altogether alien to his temperament. And, for all his love of argument, he suffered abuse with restraint and replied to the slanders of his critics with a noble silence.

Yet these Indian years were the least happy of Macaulay's life. Master of a great office and house, he was forced to maintain a state which, though held modest enough in a Member of the Supreme Council, was distasteful to a man of his simple tastes. For the dinners and routs with which the people of Calcutta endeavoured to enliven their time he felt unmitigated horror. 'Nothing can be duller,' he complained. 'Nobody speaks except to the person next him. The conversation is the most deplorable twaddle; and, as I always sit next to the lady of the highest rank, or, in other words, to the oldest, ugliest and proudest woman in the company, I am worse off than my neighbours.'

Sometimes he felt the long absence from home acutely. 'I have no words', he wrote to Ellis, 'to tell you how I pine for England, or how intensely bitter exile has been to me. I feel as if I had no other wish than to see my country again and die.' In one respect, however, he was more fortunate than many Anglo-Indians, for, though all around him rusting steel and rotting timber, mouldering books and clothes and the yellow spectral figures of his fellow Europeans marked the nature of the steaming alluvial tract in which his lot was cast, the climate affected his health very little. Indeed he found that it compared most favourably with that of the House of Commons. When it was so hot that the soldiers dressed their beefsteaks by laying them on the cannon of Fort William, Macaulay could write that he was thriving and blooming, running up and down stairs, eating and drinking heartily, and sleeping like a top. The raging sun, indeed, seemed as powerless to hurt him as the tender passion. It was his regular practice to rise at five and read for several hours before breakfast till the prattle of Hannah's baby daughter, Baba, roused him from his studies as she toddled out to him on the verandah to feed the crows with his morning toast or show him pictures. Then, after bathing in a vast tub, he would turn to the problems of the day. And in the cool of the evening, before he dined off mango fish, curry and snipe pies, with sherry, hock, and soda-water to wash them down, he would drive with his sister along the breeze-fanned, starlit bank of the Hooghly. So his days glided by in peaceful monotony.

Above all his exile was cheered by books. After the news of his sister's death he had returned to Greek literature with a passion that astonished even himself. Once he defined a scholar as one who read Plato with his feet on the fender, and in this sense he was a scholar as few men have ever been. The catalogue of his daily reading in those Indian years is remarkable. In a single fortnight he read, in the cool solitary hours before break-fast, three books of Herodotus and four plays of Aeschylus. During his exile, he went through all that was valuable in Greek and Latin literature, 'not', as he told Ellis, 'in a childish way nor in a crammy way, but understandingly judging, reperusing what is good again and skipping what I perceive to be worthless.' And always he read with his pencil at his side to mark in the margins the date of his read-ing and his comments. The historical imagination delights to picture him so – sitting, when the long Indian day was done, in the quiet of his garden till the rising moon found him with the *Philoctetes* or the *De Finibus* in his hand.

These were his more serious studies; for lighter ones he amused himself with English, French, Italian, and Spanish literature. When these proved insufficient, he taught himself Portuguese enough to be able to read Camoens with ease : 'I want no more,' he added. He used to maintain that there was no language which he could not master within four months by working ten hours a day. Annoyed by the pedantry of certain Teutonic scholars, who seemed to him unable to distinguish plausible suppositions from demonstrated truth, he spoke of learning German to confute them. 'I feel', he wrote, 'a sort of presentiment, a kind of admonition of the Deity, which assures me that the final cause of my existence – the end for which I was sent into this vale of tears – was to make game of certain Germans.'

Making fun of bad books was not the least of Macaulay's literary pleasures. On the shelves of his library – now in the possesion of the Trevelyan family – is a copy of Joseph Milner's *History of the Church*, which he bought on 31 October 1834, and read, as his pencil notes show, while in India. In the margin he kept up a kind of running commentary on the performance of the author. Before he reached page 5 he was scribbling : 'This is a stupid sermon, not a history,' nor is it easy to disagree with him. When the sententious Milner explains, 'I once for all observe here that the niceties of chronology make no part of my study in this work', Macaulay adds, 'No, nor anything else that the historian ought to attend to', and when, apparently in delirium, the pious writer breaks into a purple passage beginning, 'Hail, Tabitha, thou hast the highest glory and of the most solid kind which is attainable on earth!', he is joined by the Aristophanic chorus of his reader : 'Heyday! our historian is gone mad, I think. Hail,

Milner, thou hast written the silliest history in the worst style attainable on earth!' Sometimes the text is accompanied for several pages by a shower of 'Bahs!' and 'Trashes!', and when Milner praises an early Christian for never allowing himself to call his brother fool, his graceless critic observes, 'He never knew such a fool as Mr. Milner then!' In the end, after he had read through two and a half volumes of solemn nonsense, Macaulay for once admitted himself beaten. 'Here', he wrote, 'I give in. I have done my best. But the monotonous absurdity, dishonesty and malevolence of this man are beyond me.' It is the only recorded example of his laying down a book unfinished.

Before he had left England, Macaulay had promised Napier that he would still contribute occasionally to the *Edinburgh*, stipulating that any payment for such services now that he was so rich should not be in money but in books. Between his arrival in India and his return home, besides preparing the material for his future biographies of Clive and Hastings, he found time to write the review of Mackintosh's *History of the Revolution* and the essay on Bacon, 'prodigiously long', as he apologized to Napier, but which he thought was likely to prove popular with the many, whatever the few who knew something about it might think. As it turned out the latter didn't think much of it, and Macaulay found himself the subject of some severe criticism, for nowhere is his intellectual weakness, his almost childish impatience with the processes of abstract thought, shown to greater disadvantage than in this slashing attack on transcendental philosophy. Yet, for all his refusal to grapple with the more subtle issues of human existence there was, as his friend James Stephen wrote, something noble in his honest determination to accept nothing which he did not himself understand.

But the primary cause of Macaulay's visit to India was not literature, nor the codification of Indian law, nor the educational regeneration of the Hindu, but the business of earning and saving enough money to enable him to return to England an independent man. Life in India for its own sake had no charms for him : all the fruits of the tropics, he maintained, were not worth a pottle of Covent Garden strawberries. Helped by a favourable rate of exchange and a careful watch over his expenses he was saving, even after sending money home, six or seven thousand pounds a year from the moment he landed. 'If I live I shall get rich fast,' he wrote. 'I quite enjoy the thought of appearing in the light of an old hunks who knows on which side his bread is buttered; a warm man, a fellow who will cut up well.' It was certainly an unfamiliar rôle for Tom Macaulay. The fulfilment of his task was hastened by the death in 1837 of his Anglo-Indian uncle, General Macaulay – the uncle Colin of his youth – who left him a legacy of £10,000. He was now the master of £30,000, enough for his own needs and those of his family and sufficient, as he told a friend, to render him as independent as if he were the possessor of Burleigh or Chatsworth. Accordingly he asked to be relieved of his duties, and in December 1837 booked his passage home.

4

Parting of the Ways

I believe Macaulay to be incorruptible. You might lay ribbons, stars, garters, wealth, titles before him in vain. He has an honest, genuine love of his country, and the world would not bribe him to neglect her interests. (Sydney Smith.)

WHEN Macaulay, almost reproachfully fat, arrived home after a six months' voyage, it was to find his father dead and a much-altered England. He also found a challenge from an infuriated author, goaded into desperation by one of his characteristic reviews in the *Edinburgh*. But no duel was fought, for times were changing. At that moment the whole nation was preparing to crown its young queen, Victoria – rather a nice girl, the returned exile thought her, though her lips did part a little too much. 'London is in a strange state of excitement,' he wrote; 'the western streets are in a constant ferment. The influx of foreigners and rustics has been prodigious, and the regular inhabitants are almost as idle and as curious as the sojourners. Crowds assemble perpetually, nobody knows why, with a sort of vague expectation that there will be something to see; and, after staring at each other, disperse without seeing anything.' He felt curiously aloof from it all.

While in India, Macaulay had often turned over plans for his future life in England. In the world of books in which he had buried himself the monotonous succession of political parties had seemed strangely remote, and he, who a few years before had been thought to have the world of

Westminster at his feet, had found himself wondering at the infatuation which could lead men to exchange health, leisure and peace of mind for the fret and labour of politics. A project had been slowly forming in his mind to give his days to other and more enduring labours. Amid the pressures of a busy career, he had instructed his countrymen in the lives of some of their greatest – Milton, Dryden, Johnson, Hampden, Burleigh, Chatham; might he not now attempt a greater task which should be at once the business and amusement of his life and, forswearing parliamentary ambition, 'leave the pleasures of pestiferous rooms, sleepless nights, aching heads and diseased stomachs to Roebuck and to Praed?'

So he resolved. He would write the history of his own nation. He would begin it with the events of the Revolution of 1688, from which dated the rise of English Whiggery, and continue it till the death of George iv. Such a work would contain the story of all that Whig government had done for Great Britain – of the material and moral progress of its people, the growth of manufactures, the expansion of its empire overseas. Starting with the revolution which brought the Crown into harmony with Parliament, it would end with the revolution which brought Parliament into harmony with the nation. On Friday, 9 March 1839, in the intervals of preparing an essay on Clive for the *Edinburgh*, Macaulay wrote the first lines of his *History*.

Yet, though he had thought himself cured of that fever, the sight of Downing Street and the towers of Westminster had still the power to thrill him. In the winter following his arrival home, while travelling in Italy, he had received the offer of a minor ministerial appointment. Remembering his former slavery in such a post, he had refused. But on his return to London, where every landmark reminded him of his earlier ambitions, his resolve weakened. Moreover his party, clinging desperately to power in the face of growing Tory opposition in country and parliament, was in urgent need of his services. It was not in Macaulay's nature to decline an appeal to his loyalty. In June 1839, after an absence of six years, he re-entered the House as Liberal member for Edinburgh. Three months later Lord Melbourne invited him to join the Cabinet as Secretary-at-War. To the joy of all his friends save one or two who perceived the true nature of his genius, he laid aside his *History* for the life of politics.

It was not a very arduous office. The Tories were, of course, critical, and *The Times*, christening the new minister Mr Babbletongue Macaulay, declared that he was no more fit for office than one of her Majesty's favourite monkeys. But such strictures soon died away in the clamour of more important controversies, and the Secretary-at-War, in the piping, economical times of peace, passed his estimates without slip or criticism. His administrative experience in India had made him quieter and even conciliatory, and he rather enjoyed memorizing the complicated figures of his department. Once, in a bad speech on a Tory vote of confidence, he was shouted down, but soon recovered his reputation with a stirring oration on the majesty of the British flag (which had been getting itself into trouble in China). His patriotism was becoming a steadily more marked feature of his politics, and he declared his readiness to resign with Palmerston if the ambitions of France were not checked. At the time he was writing the essay on Warren Hastings.

Macaulay's return to politics as a Cabinet Minister, coupled with the growing fame of his writings – his articles were the mainstay of the *Edinburgh* that year – made him the lion of the London season. He knew that it was good for him for a while : he had been growing too much of a bookworm in India and on the voyage home; now he had to do his reading as he dressed for dinner. No London party in the next two years was complete without his brilliant talk, broken now, as his old friend Sydney Smith observed, by occasional flashes of silence which made it perfectly delightful. And a fellow guest at Bowood paid an amazed tribute in his diary to that roaring torrent of information, so universal and yet so good-humoured, which drowned even the joys of hearing Tom Moore sing his own 'O come to me when daylight sets,' and left a very angry Samuel Rogers without a single listener.

Macaulay's tenure of office was not a long one. All through 1840 he was standing as best he could in a swaying, falling Government, its popularity long gone, a heavy deficit on its estimates, and its capacity even to carry the smallest measure at the mercy of its opponents. Defeat, long averted, came on a debate on the Sugar Duties in the summer of 1841. The ensuing General Election, which saw Macaulay safely returned again for Edinburgh, witnessed throughout southern England a series of sweeping Tory victories. In August the ministry resigned. The would-be historian, who was already pining for release, was at liberty once more. He accepted the situation with delight. 'Now,' he wrote, 'I am free. I am independent. I am in Parliament, as honourably seated as a man can be. My family is comfortably off. I have leisure for literature; yet I am not reduced to the necessity of writing for money. If I had to choose a lot from all that there are in human life, I am not sure that I should prefer any to that which has fallen to me. I am sincerely and thoroughly contented.'

Shortly before the General Election, Trevelyan, who during his leave from India had been living in Great George Street with his brother-in-law, was to the latter's intense joy appointed to the home service as Assistant-Secretary to the Treasury. He now moved with his family to more permanent quarters at Clapham, and Macaulay took bachelor chambers on the second floor of the Albany. Here, with his walls furnished high with books, and a few yards from the thunder of Piccadilly, he was able to follow a kind of existence well-suited to his taste – college life at the West End of London, as he called it – and to devote himself to his *History*. He immediately resumed the scarcely-begun task, intending to cover during the years of opposition the period from the Revolution to the accession of the House of Hanover. 'I have at last begun my historical labours', he wrote on 5 November 1841, 'I can hardly say with how much interest and delight. I really do not think that there is in our literature so great a void as that which I am trying to supply. English history from 1688 to the French Revolution is even to educated people almost a *terra incognita*. . . . The materials for an amusing narrative are immense. I shall not be satisfied unless I produce something which shall for a few days supersede the last fashionable novel on the tables of young ladies.' To be the better equipped for his work, he resolved to visit the scenes of all the principal events to be recorded, both in the British Isles and on the Continent.

Yet, though he plunged industriously into the sea of materials awaiting him, the initial progress of the *History* was slow: after the first year's work he had only rough-hewn half of the introductory volume. There were still too many other interests claiming him: a man in the early forties who has made a conspicuous success in the triple fields of literature, politics and administration can scarcely hope to be left in peace for long. Napier in particular was insistent on the necessity for his continued support of the *Edinburgh*, and though Macaulay stipulated that the themes of his articles must have some bearing on his principal task it was not till 1845 that he could bring himself to tell him that he would write no more for him till his *History* was done. Never, he explained, could he write to please himself until the subject had driven every other thought from his head.

For some time past another interest beside those of politics and historical literature had been occupying Macaulay's mind. Far back in India, he had been fired by Perizonius's theory that the romantic tales of early Rome were derived from ballads, familiar to the great Latin historians but since perished. He had always been interested in this particular form of art – it was among his idiosyncrasies to buy every popular broadside hawked on the streets. He now formed the idea of replacing these lost ballads in traditional English metres. In the winter of 1838 he had visited Italy for the first time, seeing the year go out on the road between Rome and Naples where the Pontine Marshes spread out like the sea beneath Velletri's hill. Places whose names had been familiar to him since childhood – the Ciminian hill, Cortona lifting to heaven her diadem of towers, the proud mart of Pisa – set his pulse beating faster, till words began to form themselves in his mind, singing as they came of marching armies :

> From lordly Volaterrae,
>   Where scowls the far-famed hold
> Piled by the hands of giants
>   For godlike kings of old;
> From seagirt Populonia,
>   Whose sentinels descry
> Sardinia's snowy mountain-tops
>   Fringing the southern sky.

All the burning civic idealism of the man was kindled by

the associations that came surging through his mind, till
St Peter's dome sank behind the Capitol, and the Rome of
the Renaissance gave place to the Imperial city, and that
in its turn to the little republican town on the seven hills,
with Horatius gazing across the Tiber at the white porch
of his home on Palatinus :

> Then none was for a party;
>   Then all were for the state;
> Then the great man helped the poor,
>   And the poor man loved the great;
> Then lands were fairly portioned;
>   Then spoils were fairly sold;
> Then Romans were like brothers
>   In the brave days of old.

He wrote his ballads in odd moments, in long swinging
martial rhythms, and got his old friend Ellis to correct and
criticize them. They were published by Longmans at the
end of 1842 under the title of *Lays of Ancient Rome*.

Though Macaulay regarded the *Lays* as the trifles of his
leisure, the public took a more serious view of them. Those
who had seen only the Quaker and the middle-class
reformer in their author's ancestry had forgotten that
there was Highland blood in his veins. Here was poetry
admirably in tune with popular taste, based on emotions
which every honest man could share and borne on music so
stirring that only a very superior person could resist it. To
the people of Victorian England Macaulay's simple verses
served somewhat the same purpose as the ballads of a
former age had for the moss-troopers of the Border – a call
to patriotism and every manly virtue. They have been the
gateway through which many a boy has entered for the first
time into the heritage of English poetry.

The *Lays* received a wonderful reception. Even

Macaulay's oldest and fiercest critic John Wilson, the old 'grog-drinking, cock-fighting, cudgel-playing' Professor of Moral Philosophy at Edinburgh, hailed them with delight in *Blackwood's*, using them as a rod with which to scourge the young sentimental poets who, he declared, could never match such honest, bold stuff. In a single generation the English public absorbed a hundred thousand copies. Only Leigh Hunt, in a letter contrasting them unfavourably with *The Faerie Queene* and asking their author for money, took a less favourable view.

The publication of the *Lays* was followed by another literary venture which Macaulay had long postponed and dreaded. He had often been approached with the suggestion that he reprint in book form the *Essays* which had delighted so many in the *Edinburgh*. He had refused, on the grounds that he had written them in haste as periodical literature, to be read once and then forgotten. He would not rest his pretences to the rank of a classic on such immature work : that claim must be won by the great *History* alone. Fortunately for the pleasure of many thousands of future readers, but unhappily for his own reputation as a historian, the fates in the shape of the American publishers decided otherwise. In the then state of American law, there was nothing to prevent a New York or Boston firm from printing as many pirated copies of an English book as it chose, without the author receiving a penny of the profits or having the least say in its publication. Such was the fate of Macaulay's *Essays*. Before the end of 1842 American copies were being smuggled into England, and the question was now merely whether Macaulay and Longmans or Carey and Hart of Philadelphia should supply the English market with them.

The *Essays* were published in England in January 1843. They won instantaneous success. A second edition followed

almost immediately. Within a generation of their publication, Macaulay's nephew could write that the demand for
them had become so steady that it rose and fell like that of
coal with the general prosperity of the nation. They have
remained the popular criterion by which Macaulay is
judged; for since his day, for every thousand who have
read his *History of England*, a hundred thousand have
read his *Essays*. Like the *Lays* to lovers of poetry, they
have served admirably to introduce generations of young
readers to the study of history. Yet in the truest sense of
the word they are not history so much as popular commentary on history, and no one knew this better than their
author.

To the three beings who loved him best, the noise of
Macaulay's advancing fame never penetrated. To Margaret
– the Baba of his Indian days – George and Alice,
Hannah's children, he was merely the perfect uncle who
was always ready to lay down his work and play with
them. When George was told that his uncle Tom was
going to spend five years collecting material for a History
of England, he could only imagine that he was going to
devote his time to collecting the best pens and paper that
money could buy. His sister once recalled that of the
many people she had known who loved children Macaulay
alone never tired of being with them. These little creatures,
he felt – so gay, so like him in their enthusiasms, their
eagerness to learn and then tell impulsively all they had
learnt – were the only true poets. For their delectation, he
would pretend to be an old Jewish clothier, or crouch, a
peculiarly fierce tiger, in a den of newspapers behind the
sofa until his hunters would shriek with terror and beg
him to start again. And every Sunday he would make his
way to Clapham to spend his leisure with his little loves,
taking them for long walks across the Surrey fields of those

far pastoral days, to Blackwell eastwards or Richmond in the west.

When he was away from them Macaulay would write the children long letters, taking infinite trouble to ensure that they should charm their recipients. 'I am always glad to make my little girl happy,' he wrote to Margaret, 'and nothing pleases me so much as to see that she likes books. For when she is as old as I am, she will find that they are better than all the tarts, and cakes, and toys, and plays, and sights in the world. If anybody would make me the greatest king that ever lived, with palaces, and gardens, and fine dinners, and wine, and coaches, and beautiful clothes, and hundreds of servants, on condition that I would not read books, I would not be a king. I would rather be a poor man in a garret with plenty of books than a king who did not love reading.' It was true. And sometimes for the children's delight he would break into rhyme. 'Michaelmas,' he wrote, 'will, I hope, find us all at Clapham over a noble goose.... Do you know the beautiful Puseyite hymn on Michaelmas Day? It is a great favourite with all the Tractarians. You and Alice should learn it. It begins:

'Though Quakers scowl, though Baptists howl,
    Though Plymouth Brethren rage,
We Churchmen gay will wallow to-day
    In apple sauce, onions and sage.

'Ply knife and fork, and draw the cork,
    And have the bottle handy:
For each slice of goose will introduce
    A thimbleful of brandy.'

Is it not good? I wonder who the author can be. Not Newman, I think. It is above him. Perhaps it is Bishop

Wilberforce.' He was always particularly careful to provide for great occasions – birthdays, traditional festivals, and holidays – some special mark of his love. 'Alice' he recorded in his journal 'was in perfect raptures over her Valentine. She begged quite pathetically to be told the truth about it. When we were alone, she said : "I am going to be very serious." Down she fell before me on her knees and lifted up her hands : "Dear uncle, do tell the truth to your little girl. Did you send the Valentine?" I did not choose to tell a real lie to a child, even about such a trifle, and so I owned to it.'

As the children grew older Macaulay changed his Homeric games with them for more serious occupations. There would be visits to the Chinese Museum and the new Zoological Gardens, to the Colosseum in Regent's Park and Madame Tussaud's Chamber of Horrors, and, most delightful of all, intimate, absorbing walks through the City while Uncle Tom poured out an endless stream of historical reminiscence, peopling every alley and doorway with fascinating romantic creatures. On such occasions they would lunch with him first in his rooms in the Albany, as they did on a January day in 1845, off fowl, ham, marrow-bones, tart, olives and champagne, before proceeding, a little portentously, to the National Gallery.

With such a background to life Macaulay did not take the duties of parliamentary opposition very seriously. He spoke seldom, and when he did so it was always on a subject on which he felt himself an authority. His most notable effort – and a fine example of the way in which a sincere man with knowledge and with no axe of his own to grind can sway an assembly which respects him – was in the debates on the law of copyright. Here he was instrumental in persuading the House to reject a measure, prompted by a wave of popular sentiment, which would have been unduly favourable to authors at the expense of the reading public; later he was equally successful in ridding a revised bill of clauses which would have pressed hard on the dependents of dead writers. He was becoming recognized everywhere as the ambassador of literature among men of affairs.

In December 1845 Sir Robert Peel, confronted with the threat of Irish famine, resolved that the Corn Laws – which his party had been returned four years before to defend – must be repealed. In the alarms and excursions that followed, Macaulay was present at the consultations of the Whig shadow Cabinet – an experience not without value to one engaged in the description of the revolutions of a previous age. On 19 December, Lord John Russell was sent for by the Queen, and Macaulay described in a letter to his sister the excitements of that day. 'It is an odd thing to see a Ministry making. I never witnessed the process before. Lord John has been all day in his inner library. His ante-chamber has been filled with comers and goers, some talking in knots, some writing notes at tables. Every five minutes somebody is called into the inner room. As the people who have been closeted come out, the cry of the whole body of expectants is, "What are you?" ' Macaulay himself was summoned at once and offered the Pay Office, a post allowing sufficient leisure for him to accept. But next night as he was undressing, there was a knock on the door of his chambers, and he learnt that all was over: Russell, confronted by a quarrel between Palmerston and Lord Grey, had failed to form a Ministry and had handed the poisoned chalice back to Sir Robert. 'We stayed in when we ought to have gone out, and now we stay out when we ought to have gone in,' was Macaulay's scornful comment. Next morning in the Albany he returned to his *History*.

The respite was short-lived. On the night of 26 June
1846, the Act that repealed the Corn Laws passed the
Lords, and the Tories divided in bitter antagonism, were
defeated in the Commons. A few days later Macaulay took
the oaths as Paymaster-General. The post gave him plenty
of leisure, and, beyond signing pensions and attending
Board meetings in Chelsea Hospital, he had little to do to
earn his £2,000 a year. Every spare moment he continued to give to the preparation of his *History* : he was
deep now in the tale of Monmouth's Rebellion. But as a
Minister, his nights had to be spent in the House of
Commons and, though he would not recognize it, he was
beginning to overwork himself. Once, in a debate on the
Ten Hours Bill, he spoke in his old manner – a glorious
speech in which enduring principles drawn from history
were used to illustrate the practical necessities of the
moment. 'Man,' he declared with a look of contempt at
those who held that a few hours of enforced rest for the
labourer must ruin the country, 'man is the great instru-
ment that produces wealth. . . . We are not poorer, but
richer, because we have, through many ages, rested from
labour one day in seven. That day is not lost. While
industry is suspended, while the plough lies in the furrow,
while the Exchange is silent, while no smoke ascends from
the factory, a process is going on quite as important to the
wealth of nations as any process which is performed on
more busy days. Man, the machine of machines, the
machine compared with which all the contrivances of the
Watts and the Arkwrights are worthless, is repairing and
winding up, so that he returns to his labours on the
Monday with clearer intellect, with livelier spirits, with
renewed corporal vigour. Never will I believe that what
makes a population stronger and healthier and wiser and
better, can ultimately make it poorer.'

In the summer of 1847 there was a general election. The fortunes of the Whig party were high and it was expected that it would win many seats from the Tories. Macaulay went down to his own constituency at Edinburgh to seek the re-election which had always, throughout his political career, seemed so automatic. He received a rude awakening.

For some years past he had steadily been losing popularity with his constituents. His visits to them had been few and it seemed to them, when he was with them, that his chief desire was to leave them as soon as possible. They began to assume that he was more concerned with his historical and literary labours than with their interests. When they wrote to him, he failed to answer their letters, and when they sent him delegations it was he, not they, who did the talking. But there were other and more serious differences between them and their representative. His views on constituency finance were altogether too high-planed for their taste. When they asked him to subscribe to a race cup, he replied curtly that he had nothing to waste on gaieties which at the very best could only be considered harmless. Frugalities, which to him seemed the unquestioning commonplace of Liberal principle, to them seemed only mean. 'In return for your generous confidence,' he told them, 'I offer Parliamentary service and nothing else.' Most constituencies expect something more.

Against Macaulay's candidature there now gathered a formidable combination. With his Tory opponents were allied those of his own party whom his sins of omission had offended, and a strange miscellany of clericals of divers sects who hated his uncompromising spirit of toleration, and found a common plank against him in the slogan of 'Christian men ought to send Christian men to represent them.' Two other elements added their strength to the opposition – those who loved to drink their whisky cheap and were angered by Macaulay's refusal to vote against the spirit duties, and the mob which, though it had no vote had a lusty voice and detested the proud Whig who had urged the House to refuse a hearing to the People's Charter.

For a week Edinburgh was full of broadsides and ballad-singers and shouting crowds. On the morning of 30 July 1847, Macaulay watched the counting of the votes in the Merchants' Hall. Hour by hour he saw the figures mounting against him. By the afternoon he knew there was no hope. That night, while the rabble was celebrating his defeat in the fire-lit streets, Macaulay behind the shutters of his room was struggling to put the contending emotions of his heart to paper :

The day of tumult, strife, defeat, was o'er;
    Worn out with toil, and noise, and scorn, and spleen,
I slumbered, and in slumber saw once more
    A room in an old mansion, long unseen.

That room, methought, was curtained from the light;
    Yet through the curtains shone the moon's cold ray
Full on a cradle, where, in linen white,
    Sleeping life's first soft sleep, an infant lay.

And lo! the fairy queens who rule our birth
    Drew nigh to speak the new-born baby's doom :
With noiseless step, which left no trace on earth,
    From gloom they came, and vanished into gloom.

Not deigning on the boy a glance to cast
    Swept careless by the gorgeous Queen of Gain;
More scornful still the Queen of Fashion passed,
    With mincing gait and sneer of cold disdain.

The Queen of Power tossed high her jewelled head,
    And o'er her shoulder threw a wrathful frown.
The Queen of Pleasure on the pillow shed
    Scarce one stray rose-leaf from her fragrant crown.

Still Fay in long procession followed Fay;
    And still the little couch remained unblest :
But, when those wayward sprites had passed away,
    Came One, the last, the mightiest, and the best.

Oh glorious lady, with the eyes of light,
    And laurels clustering round thy lofty brow,
Who by the cradle's side didst watch that night,
    Warbling a sweet strange music, who wast thou?

'Yes, darling; let them go,' so ran the strain :
    'Yes; let them go, gain, fashion, pleasure, power,
And all the busy elves to whose domain
    Belongs the nether sphere, the fleeting hour.

'Without one envious sigh, one anxious scheme,
    The nether sphere, the fleeting hour resign,
Mine is the world of thought, the world of dream,
    Mine all the past, and all the future mine.

'Fortune, that lays in sport the mighty low,
    Age, that to penance turns the joys of youth,
Shall leave untouched the gifts which I bestow,
    The sense of beauty and the thirst of truth.

'Of the fair brotherhood who share my grace,
    I, from thy natal day, pronounce thee free;
And, if for some I keep a nobler place,
    I keep for none a happier than for thee.

57

'Yes; thou wilt love me with exceeding love;
  And I will tenfold all that love repay :
Still smiling, though the tender may reprove,
  Still faithful, though the trusted may betray.

'In the dark hour of shame, I deigned to stand
  Before the frowning peers at Bacon's side :
On a far shore I smoothed with tender hand,
  Through months of pain, the sleepless bed of Hyde;

'I brought the wise and brave of ancient days
  To cheer the cell where Raleigh pined alone :
I lighted Milton's darkness with the blaze
  Of the bright ranks that guard the eternal throne.

'And even so, my child, it is my pleasure
  That thou not then alone shouldst feel me nigh,
When in domestic bliss and studious leisure
  Thy weeks uncounted come, uncounted fly;

'No : when on restless night dawns cheerless morrow,
  When weary soul and wasting body pine,
Thine am I still, in danger, sickness, sorrow,
  In conflict, obloquy, want, exile, thine.'

Fate at last had decided his destiny for him.

5

The Great History

Until quite recent times, from the days of Clarendon down through Gibbon, Carlyle and Macaulay to Green and Lecky, historical writing was not merely the mutual conversation of scholars with one another, but was the means of spreading far and wide throughout all the reading classes a love and knowledge of history, an elevated and critical patriotism, and certain qualities of mind and heart.
(G. M. Trevelyan, *Clio: A Muse.*)

WITHOUT a further thought for the past, Macaulay turned to the future. Henceforward he would live in a citadel of his own making : and all attempts to beguile him from it on to the perilous plains of public life would be in vain. 'Having once been manumitted, after the old fashion, by a slap in the face,' he told Ellis, 'I shall not take to bondage again.' Among his books a great task was awaiting him.

To that task he now gave himself. For its achievement no toil could be too great. He was writing from materials now, not, as in the past with his essays, merely from that superb memory. To the making of every paragraph went the reading of perhaps a score of books and a hundred pamphlets, correspondence with the possessors of facts and figures which could not be gleaned from the printed page – foreign antiquaries, custodians of manuscripts, registrars of births and burials – and often a visit to some obscure or remote spot which he was describing. We see him in his

diary toiling up the slope of Killiecrankie, testing the time
the English army took to climb the pass, or knocking at
the doors of Londonderry cottages to enquire of aged
inhabitants traditions of the siege told them by their
fathers, and filling all the while his teeming notebooks.
Most of all we picture him in that book-lined upper room
in the Albany, working from seven in the morning till
seven at night, or surrounded by pamphlets in the King's
Library in the British Museum.

Out of such labour, ungrudgingly and lovingly given,
arises the never-failing interest of his narrative. He never
mentions a person or place in the course of his many
thousand pages without bringing them before his readers
in a few telling words. His minor characters, whether
accurate or not, are as alive and convincing as Shakespeare's.
The obscure plotter Ferguson, with 'his broad Scotch ac-
cent, his tall and lean figure, his lantern jaws, the gleam of
his sharp eyes, his cheeks inflamed by an eruption, his
shoulders deformed', is drawn as carefully as William or
Marlborough. Yet all the while the artist is selecting, not
from his own imagination but from painfully garnered
stores of knowledge. 'Not to the ant nor to the spider, but
to the bee that collects materials from far and wide and
transmutes them into honey,' Macaulay loved – borrowing
Bacon's words – to compare the historian at his work.
Those who follow the easy rapid march of his pages tend
to forget 'the wonderful industry, the honest, humble,
previous toil of this great scholar*'. All the time he was
going ahead of his narrative with axe and spade, exploring
and preparing the ground.

No printed source did he neglect. Some will recall the
paragraph in which he describes the wild life of the English
countryside in 1685 :

* Thackeray.

The red deer were then as common in Gloucestershire and Hampshire as they now are among the Grampian Hills. On one occasion Queen Anne, travelling to Portsmouth, saw a herd of no less than five hundred. The wild bull with his white mane was still to be found wandering in a few of the southern forests. The badger made his dark and tortuous hole on the side of every hill where the copsewood grew thick. The wild cats were frequently heard by night wailing round the lodges of the rangers of Whittlebury and Needwood. The yellow-breasted marten was still pursued in Cranborne Chase for his fur, reputed inferior only to that of the sable. Fen eagles, measuring more than nine feet between the extremities of the wings, preyed on fish along the coast of Norfolk. On all the downs, from the British Channel to Yorkshire, huge bustards strayed in troops of fifty or sixty, and were often hunted with greyhounds. The marshes of Cambridgeshire and Lincolnshire were covered during some months of every year by immense clouds of cranes.

At the foot of that page he gives his authorities for this beautiful passage, subsidiary altogether to the main purposes of his narrative – White's *Selborne*; Bell's *History of British Quadrupeds*; *Gentleman's Recreation*, 1686; Aubrey's *Natural History of Wiltshire*, 1685; Morton's *History of Northamptonshire*, 1712; *Willoughby's Ornithology* by Ray, 1678; Latham's *General Synopsis of Birds*; and Sir Thomas Browne's *Account of Birds found in Norfolk*. Few of the professional historians of a later age have possessed a culture wide enough to enrich their readers with such unusual treasure. The same width of reading increases the panorama of Macaulay's *History* at every turn : when he describes the assault on Namur in July 1695 he remembers to add, in a footnote, that it was here that Captain Shandy received the memorable wound in his groin.

In particular Macaulay made himself master of contemporary pamphlets and journalism, soaking his mind, as he put it, in the transitory literature of the day. He sought after seventeenth-century pamphlets as a terrier seeks rats, pursuing them on sunny afternoons on Holborn bookstalls and devouring them, even on a visit to Windsor Castle, as he sat in his bedroom by a blazing January fire. And no man before his day ever had such an acquaintance with that great treasury of *Flying Posts*, *Postboys*, and *Posts* in the Newspaper Room at the British Museum. In their company he learnt to grow familiar with the habits and ways of thinking of a past generation.

Exploring country which was then virgin, Macaulay naturally fell into many errors. Pamphlets and contemporary newspapers are seldom written in an entirely disinterested and non-partisan manner, and in the later seventeenth century, party feeling ran to criminal heights. Honest nineteenth-century Whig that he was, Macaulay was too ready to take at their face-value tales emanating from the republican printing presses during the last years of the Stuart regime from which he would have drawn back in horror had he been better acquainted with the past histories and characters of those who wrote them. But the *bona fides* of anonymous journalists and pamphleteers is not to be found impressed on their products; it must be sought for in the tangled forests of commentary, good and bad, passed on them by those who had the best means of judging them – their contemporaries. And such judgement is more often reposited in manuscript letters than in print.

Unfortunately, at the time that Macaulay wrote, access to old letters, at once the most intimate and reliable of all sources of historical information, was not easy to come by. The vast collections of private correspondence, since then calendared and opened to the student by the labours of the Historical Manuscripts Commission and of various antiquarian societies, were still lying neglected and un-sorted in country-house attics and muniment rooms, while the great manuscript treasuries of the British Museum, Record Office, and Bodleian were known only to a few laborious and leisured scholars. To a busy man, who had spent the best part of his life in public affairs, they were almost *terra incognita*. When it is remembered that even so commonplace a source as Luttrell's *Brief Relation* was only available to Macaulay at the expense of a lengthy visit to All Souls at Oxford and of many weary hours poring over the cramped and illegible writing of the original, the handicap under which he worked compared with that of modern scholars becomes apparent. When he endeavoured to consult the Tanner and Wharton Mss in the Bodleian – a place in which he said he could spend ten years without a moment's ennui – he was rung out by the bored attendants punctually at three every afternoon. At the time when Macaulay was working, English historical scholarship was at its lowest ebb. Those who blame him for his neglect of documents might as justly censure Napoleon for failing to use machine-guns at Waterloo. There is something almost pathetic in the delight with which he announces Lord Spencer's permission for him to 'rummage' in the library at Althorp or the arrival of Lord Denbigh's manuscripts at the British Museum. Such publications as the *Verney Papers* and *Pepys's Diary*, then only available in an abbreviated and garbled form, he devoured greedily; the latter even formed the subject of a nightmare, in which little Alice appeared to him with a penitential face and confessed that she had forged it. 'What!' he had cried in his horror, 'I have been quoting in reviews, and in my *History*, a forgery of yours as a book of the highest authority! How shall I ever hold up my head again.' He awoke with the fright of it, Alice's supplicating voice still in his ears.

Macaulay's ignorance of contemporary correspondence necessarily vitiates the value of much of his *History*. Through it his sense of historical proportion is distorted. A printed fable or libel, invented long after the time to which it refers, is allowed to appear in his pages because he was unaware of the contemporary letters which prove its falsehood. Thus Locke's expulsion from Christ Church is painted entirely from the viewpoint of his later Whig eulogists without the correction provided by the correspondence of his Oxford contemporary, Dr Prideaux, who reveals that the Whig philosopher fled voluntarily to Holland on the discovery of the Rye House Plot. Macaulay's statement that no officer of the Restoration Navy who was versed in sea affairs was also a gentleman, though partly true, becomes untenable in the light of the Dartmouth or Portland papers, and his picture of the seventeenth-century Londoner as a species apart from the rest of the nation is unbelievable to anyone acquainted with the contents of any considerable country-house Mss collection, with its revelation of how close was the relationship between a London merchant and his country brothers and cousins.

Perhaps the most startling result of Macaulay's lack of familiarity with the letters of his period appears in his treatment of the country gentleman – 'the gross, uneducated, untravelled country gentleman', with hardly 'learning enough to sign his name to a *Mittimus*', and generally, of course, a Tory. The present writer has perused many thousands of letters written by seventeenth-century squires, great and small, and scarcely remembers a single one which marks its author as anything but an educated and cultured man. Certain decencies and refinements requisite in the society of a later age these village lords lacked, but in all that denotes true civilization they were more often than not the superiors of their nineteenth-century descendants. Had Macaulay used his eyes in this instance, he might have to some extent corrected himself: statements that the squire of 1685 troubled himself little about decorating his abode and, if he attempted to do so, produced only deformity, or that his library consisted of little more than *Hudibras, Baker's Chronicle, Tarlton's Jests*, and the *Seven Champions of Christendom*, come strangely from the pen of a conscientious man who could see with his own eyes Sudbury, Belton, or Lyme. The truth is that Macaulay's intimate knowledge of the literature of Augustan England led him astray. Only great Literature reflects reality; often it deliberately distorts and caricatures.

Yet the writing of his *History of England* made Macaulay a historian. Of technical training for his task he had had scarcely any, for there was then scarcely any to be had. His studies at school and university had been strictly classical, his lot since then had been cast in the world of affairs, and such historical knowledge as he possessed was the result of the immense but quite un-directed reading of his leisure hours. For his introductory chapters leading up to the events of the Revolution – the real point at which he had resolved to begin his labours – he relied, as he had done in his *Essays*, solely on that general reading and on his memory. The relation in Volume I of the Civil Wars and the reign of Charles II abounds with common errors. Lucy Walter becomes Lucy Walters; Ormonde, who was governing Ireland, is made to follow his son Ossory, who died in London, to the grave; and the London Whigs of 1683 are declared to be more prosperous than their opponents, when in fact the wealthier citizens of that date were more often Tories. It was not till he reached the year 1685 that Macaulay began to rely on something more solid and reliable than general reading and common report, nor till his own defeat at Edinburgh that he became free to devote himself whole-heartedly to the search for such materials. The sources from which he derives his account of the death of Charles II are admirable, and include nearly all those which were available at the time he wrote. Thereafter, he steadily improved as an historian.

For the student of history Macaulay's great work begins with that famous third chapter, written during the year 1848, in which he takes a mountain survey of England at the time of James II's accession. It is in his feeling for the nation as a whole, and not merely for the high political movements and personages of conventional history, that he is a pioneer. If anyone had preceded him in this, it was a poet and a novelist, Walter Scott, whose works he had loved in his boyhood. Macaulay was the first professed historian to think that changes in the state of a people were as important as those in a dynasty or ministry. Twenty years before, in his 'Essay on History', he had defined the perfect historian as one 'in whose work the character and spirit of an age is exhibited in miniature. . . . He shows us the court, the camp, and the senate. But he shows us also the nation.' In his third chapter Macaulay attempted to do this. He drew England in its entirety – London, the streets of Bristol, the little country town, the wild moors and marshes of the north. Errors of detail, and sometimes errors of greater moment, he commits, but he makes his readers see England as it was, and, seeing it, love it. His genius was that he felt that poetry and hidden life of the nation behind the façade of high statesmanship and the records of the great.

Indeed, it was largely a consciousness of these things that impelled him to write at all. Politician as he was, he

never forgot that the purpose of all politics was to safe-
guard the household gods and the household virtues of the
plain man – 'the fireside, the nursery, the social table, the
quiet bed'. A sense of the individual citizen's private gain
is never absent from his *History* : in all he records, one
feels the presence of Time with progress in her womb. He
cannot describe the scene of Argyll's rebellion without
remembering with joy that the streams which then held
their quiet course through moors and sheepwalks now flow
through prosperous towns and turn the wheels of factories.
He loves to contrast the material plenty of the artisan of
his own day with the squalid poverty of the peasant of
former centuries. Sometimes in doing so he misses the
true purport of his subject : it is an error in historians to
contrast the past too emphatically with their own present,
lest they fall into the fault of seeing the former only
through the eyes of the latter. When Macaulay described
the Highlanders of the seventeenth century as barbarians
because their food and housing differed from his own he
was committing that mistake.

Yet imagination is so rare a gift in the recorder of
history who, having to be his own dryasdust, is often
unable to raise his eyes from the paper in front of him, that
we gladly forgive Macaulay his faults. Monmouth's defeated army pouring at dawn through the streets of
Bridgwater, the night of terror in London after James's
flight, the Jacobite conspirators drinking together in the
tavern in Spring Garden, have the very impress of living
transient emotion, given by the genius of their recorder an
eternal form. 'To recover some of our ancestors' real
thoughts and feelings', it has been finely said, 'is the
hardest, subtlest and most educative function that the
historian can perform.'* It is this which Macaulay succeeds

* G. M. Trevelyan, *Clio: A Muse.*

supremely in doing. In that noble passage which describes the little cemetery of St Peter's Chapel in the Tower – 'no sadder spot on earth' – all the sympathy and tender mercy of a great heart is given to the service of history.

Faults he has, many and grave. The splendid rhetoric that carries his reader on to so many heights too often distorts the truth or conceals the awkward fact which would spoil it. Macaulay the politician was not in this respect helpful to Macaulay the historian : the evil fruit of the hustings too often beguiled him. The natural vigour of his temperament had always caused him to see men and their motives too much in black and white, and the habits of party oratory tended to intensify still more these lights and shades. So he must paint James wholly bad and William wholly good; so he must contrast Marlborough's genius – 'the red coat and eagle eye of the victor of Blenheim',* which he never lived to draw – against the black shade of unbroken avarice and treachery. To this rhetoric his natural ear for fine-sounding synthesis the more inclined him. He who cared little for music when he heard it in a concert room loved it in words and could never resist its charm. A kind of literary Pied Piper always went before him, sometimes leading him far from the paths of sober reality.

And sometimes it led him into great crimes against the Muse of History. It was wrong to tell of Kirke a foul and horrible story which a few lines on he admits he did not believe, for once told, as Macaulay well knew, the prejudice against Kirke was doubled. It was worse to use all the artistry of which he was so supreme a master to turn the eyes of his readers from William's inescapable responsibility for the cold-blooded massacre of Glencoe – a more foul tyranny against the subject than any perpetrated

* G. M. Trevelyan, *Clio: A Muse.*

by a Stuart King. It was consciously dishonest to strengthen the charges against Marlborough by retailing as certain fact unproved libels taken from obscure Jacobite papers which he himself regarded as hopelessly unreliable on every other subject.

It was more venial in Macaulay to allow a natural preference for Whigs to Tories to colour his judgements. A man cannot rightly enter into the spirit of an age in which two great forms of thought and feeling struggle for mastery if he is not able to share one or other of them; unless he be a god, he cannot well share both. Macaulay saw the seventeenth century from the standpoint of Whig ideals and emotions, as did also, in their different ways, Cromwell and Milton and Russell; he is none the worse an historian for doing so. Yet the fallibility of even a good man's nature has seldom been more clearly shown than in the quite unconscious manner in which he applied one standard of judgements to the conduct of his own party and quite another to that of his opponents. The old Cromwellian Rumbold, who plotted to murder Charles and James as they drove by unarmed in their coach, merely bore 'a part from which he would have shrunk with horror if his clear understanding had not been overclouded and his manly heart corrupted by party spirit'. No such excuses are made for Jacobite would-be assassins. When Charles II is blamed for yielding to the pressure of Parliament to pass 'odious acts against the separatists', one is left with the feeling that it is only wrong for a king to refuse assent to a measure presented to him by both Houses when that measure is a Whig one. Nothing could provide a greater contrast than Macaulay's somewhat heartless relation of the treatment of the helpless Clerkenwell monks at the hand of the London mob with the indignation with which he refers to the situation of the Protestants in Catholic

Ireland – 'unarmed in the midst of an armed and hostile population'. Occasionally this partisanship leads Macaulay into a surprising degree of blindness. In the pages he devotes to making such exquisite fun of the non-jurors' reasoning powers, he altogether misses sight of the simple fact that they remained true to the King whose bread they had eaten, not out of any reason, but out of plain loyalty. Nor, English though he is, does Macaulay in his zest for the Whig cause seem aware of the disgrace which hundreds of thousands of his countrymen felt at the spectacle of a Dutch army marching in triumph across England.

Yet when all is said and done, Macaulay was too honest a man to be perpetually unjust, even to Tories. He had, as he once said of Cromwell, 'a high, stout, honest, English heart', and like his own ranks of Tuscany, he could scarce forbear to cheer at whatever struck him as noble in his opponents. The non-juror Ken receives as liberal a meed of praise as any man can earn from another : 'His intellect was indeed darkened by many superstitions and prejudices, but his moral character, when impartially reviewed, sustains a comparison with any in ecclesiastical history and seems to approach, as near as human infirmity permits, to the ideal perfection of Christian virtue.' Nor could he find it in his heart to censure the behaviour of a stout Tory prelate who offered his coach-horses to draw the royal artillery into action at Sedgemoor – conduct which he observes has 'with strange inconsistency been condemned by some Whig writers who can see nothing criminal in the conduct of the numerous Puritan ministers then in arms against the government'. Macaulay's capacity for entering into the feelings of a foe is proved by his lines on a Jacobite's grave, written when he was first gathering materials for his *History* :

Rothley Temple, Macaulay's birthplace.

An early portrait of Macaulay.

Detail from a painting by Sir George Hayter entitled 'The House of Commons 1833 Moving the Address to the Crown'. Macaulay (*circled*) is on the left-hand side of the picture.

OPPOSITE PAGE
Hannah Trevelyan, Macaulay's sister and closest friend.
A portrait of Macaulay painted in 1849 by J. Patridge.

Holly Lodge, Campden Hill, Macaulay's home from 1856 until his death in 1859.

Sketch of Macaulay's funeral in Westminster Abbey by G. Scharf.

The Funeral of Lord Macaulay.
Sketched by G. Scharf in Westminster Abbey.
January 9th 1860.

To my true king I offered free from stain
Courage and faith; vain faith, and courage vain.
For him, I threw lands, honours, wealth, away,
And one dear hope, that was more prized than they.
For him I languished in a foreign clime,
Grey-haired with sorrow in my manhood's prime;
Heard on Lavernia Scargill's whispering trees,
And pined by Arno for my lovelier Tees;
Beheld each night my home in fevered sleep,
Each morning started from the dream to weep;
Till God, who saw me tried too sorely, gave
The resting place I asked, an early grave.
Oh thou, whom chance leads to this nameless stone,
From that proud country which was once mine own,
By those white cliffs I never more must see,
By that dear language which I spake like thee,
Forget all feuds and shed one English tear
O'er English dust. A broken heart lies here.

He loved the Whig cause and those who fought for it, but he loved England more.

But above all others of his countrymen who have written history, Macaulay was in two respects pre-eminent. Unlike those professional historians who pursue the sheltered life of academies, he was a man of affairs : he had mixed in the great world he described, knew the motives and temptations of public men and the difficulties of those in place. Gibbon had found that the captain of Hampshire militia was not useless to the historian of the Roman Empire; in a greater measure Macaulay was aided by the member for Calne and Leeds, the Indian Administrator, the Secretary-at-War. He knew that rakes will sometimes achieve by acquired tact great combinations beyond the reach of orators and philosophers, that the common people are more loyal than their leaders, that 'in every age the vilest specimens of human nature are to be found among the demagogues'. Many who write history with extreme fidelity to documentary evidence do not know these things, and carry their readers for lack of such knowledge into a world of unreality.

Even more rare in a historian than his knowledge of the world were the pains which Macaulay took to make his story readable. History must be, he held, no mere accumulation of isolated facts for the benefit of a few secluded scholars : it must be the proper narration and interpretation of those facts for the education and delight of mankind. To hurry as fast as possible over what was dull and to dwell as long as possible on whatever could be made picturesque and dramatic was part of the historian's business. And to achieve lucidity no effort must be spared. 'What trouble these few pages have cost me', he wrote; 'the great object is that, after all this trouble, they may read it as if they had been spoken and flow as easily as table-talk.' When from his crowded note-books he had stored his memory with the needful materials, he would draft a passage at white heat : then he would set to work, with infinite care and endless erasions, to remodel his first hieroglyphics into a more perfect form. Of this 'fair copy' he made it his duty to complete six or seven foolscap sheets regularly each day, never continuing after the fine edge was off his zest for writing lest his own weariness might communicate itself to his readers. When his paragraph or chapter was done he would return to it again, calling in the Trevelyans or his friend Ellis to criticize, and recasting it sometimes a dozen times before he was satisfied. The easy and restless flow of his narrative from sentence to sentence and paragraph to paragraph arises less from natural fluency than from his determination to give to this, the supreme work of his life, nothing but the very best. 'At all events,' he wrote, 'I have aimed high; I have tried to do something that may be remembered; I have had the year 2000, and even the year 3000, often in my mind; I have sacrified nothing to temporary fashions of thought and style; and, if I fail, my failure will be more honourable than nine-tenths of the successes I have witnessed.'

Everything now was subordinated to the business of bringing the first part of his task to completion. The scenes of his labours had become the setting of his entire life – the paper-strewn table in his room in the Albany, the Museum and the library of the Athenæum, and the pleasant places he visited in his historical pilgrimages: Glencoe's light and shade, Duke Humphrey's library above the trees of Exeter garden, and the water meadows round Derry. Even the holidays he took each spring with the Trevelyans were fitted to the same inexorable purpose, though he never failed to combine his own acquisition of knowledge with the instruction and entertainment of his nephew and nieces. Then, when the day's journey was done, as they walked by the pool beneath Lichfield's cathedral or through the rows of Chester, that inexhaustible energy would be seen at its highest as he poured out, to the delight of his companions, a flow of never-ceasing and cheerful commentary on the historical scenes about them.

Throughout the year 1848 the first part of the great work went rapidly forward towards completion. By the end of October he was grappling with proofs and writing that in a few weeks his labours would begin to lighten. On 18 November he was able to relax and, noting in his journal that he would henceforward record his meals as honest Pepys did, entertained Ellis to dinner on lobster

curry, woodcock and macaroni. Ten days later the advance
copies of Volumes I and II, carrying his tale down to 1688,
were in his hands, and he had nothing to do but await the
result. 'I have armed myself', he wrote, 'with all my
philosophy for the event of a failure.'

The suspense did not last long. Before the day of
publication the first three thousand copies had been sold,
and Longmans were at work on a new edition. At the end
of January 1849, thirteen thousand had been printed, and
by May the book had reached its fifth edition. No historical
work of its importance had ever had such success, nor, indeed, scarcely any other publication. Everyone from the old
Duke of Wellington downwards was reading and praising
it. The reviewers were almost unanimous in their approval.
But perhaps what most pleased its author, who confessed
himself half afraid of such unwonted popularity, was the
testimony of a group of humble Yorkshire folk who voted
him thanks for having written a book which working men
could understand. Across the Atlantic its success – though
here Macaulay could not share even a penny – was even
more phenomenal. Four months after publication, Messrs
Harpers of New York wrote to inform him that they had
sold forty thousand copies, and that the total American
sale before the end of the year would probably exceed two
hundred thousand. Piracy on so vast a scale was unpre-
cedented, even in the New World. And Mr Crump,
another American, wrote offering Macaulay 500 dollars if
he would introduce the name of Crump into his next
volume. The Cabinet Minister, the Indian Councillor, the
Edinburgh reviewer had become merged in something
greater and more significant – the crowning lion of the
Victorian universe, a household word. 'I have seen,'
Macaulay wrote after a visit to the zoo, 'the hippopotamus,
both asleep and awake; and I can assure you he is the

ugliest of the works of God. Imagine Alderman Humphrey, stripped naked, smeared with soot, and crawling on all fours after a turtle dinner, and you have the very thing. But you must hear of my triumphs. Two damsels were just about to pass that doorway which we, on Monday, in vain attempted to enter, when I was pointed out to them. "Mr. Macaulay!" cried the lovely pair. "Is that Mr. Macaulay? Never mind the hippopotamus!" '

There were also other and more formal honours. In March 1849 he was installed as Lord Rector of the University of Glasgow and given the Freedom of the city. In July came a summons from Prince Albert to the Palace and the offer of the new Regius Chair of History at Cambridge, not unnaturally declined by one who had set his freedom before a seat in the Cabinet and £2,500 a year. 'My temper is that of the wolf in the fable,' he wrote : 'I cannot bear the collar. I have got rid of a much finer collar than this.' A later mark of esteem which both amused and pleased him was his election in January 1850 as a Bencher of Lincoln's Inn. Everywhere he was hailed as the master educator of his age. He was even privileged to instruct his sovereign, who at dinner at Buckingham Palace spoke to him of his book and confessed that she had nothing to say for her poor ancestor, James II. 'Not your Majesty's ancestor,' interposed Macaulay, 'your Majesty's predecessor.' The correction was graciously accepted. Such humility was universal.

Yet perhaps the humblest person concerned was Macaulay himself. For if his *History* in the eyes of his countrymen outsoared all others, it fell immeasurably below the perfect and unwritten history which he himself was ever trying to achieve. 'I have never read again', he wrote, 'the most popular passages of my work without painfully feeling how far my execution has fallen short of the standard which is in my mind.' On the very day that the success of his book was first assured, he turned in all humility to the work of that greater historian whom he had learnt to love and venerate in his youth, Thucydides. 'Others', he confessed, 'one may hope to match: him never.'

For such a man there could be no resting on his laurels. The first two volumes had been launched, and the narrative carried to 1688; but before the historian lay the whole ocean of the eighteenth century still to be traversed. His experience had taught him much, and, like all true artists, he was ready to learn and profit by it. 'I have now,' he wrote on 8 February 1849, 'made up my mind to change my plan about my *History*. I will first set myself the whole subject: to get, by reading and travelling, a full acquaintance with William's reign. I reckon that it will take me eighteen months to do this. I must visit Holland, Belgium, Scotland, Ireland, France. The Dutch archives and French archives must be ransacked. I will see whether anything is to be got from other diplomatic collections. I must see Londonderry, the Boyne, Aghrim, Limerick, Kinsale, Namur again, Landen, Steinkirk. I must turn over hundreds, thousands, of pamphlets. Lambeth, the Bodleian, and the other Oxford libraries, the Devonshire Papers, the British Museum, must be explored, and notes made: and then I shall go to work. When the materials are ready and the *History* mapped out in my mind, I ought easily to write on an average two of my pages daily. In two years from the time I begin writing I shall have more than finished my second part. Then I reckon a year for polishing, retouching, and printing.'

On these further labours he now embarked. 'My task', 'Did my task', 'My task and something over', is the constant refrain of his journal during the next two years.

The profits which his initial success had brought him made little difference to his way of life : indeed, they made little to his wealth, for if the royalties he received were large, the obligations with which their repute endowed him almost outweighed them. Such responsibilities he made no attempt to escape; if he did not care to live like a prince, he could at least give like one. In this luxury he indulged frequently, and after his kind, secretly. Long parted friends, stray acquaintances who had no conceivable claim on his generosity, even complete strangers who wrote to urge the needs of a common humanity, found in him an inexhaustible giver. 'I got a letter from—,' runs one typical entry in his journal, 'who is in great distress about his son's debt. I am vexed and sorry, but I wrote, insisting on being allowed to settle the matter; and I was pleased that (though there have been, and will be, other calls on me) I made this offer from the heart and with the wish to have it accepted.' Sometimes the demands he suffered from those who got wind of his generosity were startling. 'What strange begging letters I do receive!' he wrote on one occasion. 'A fellow has written to me telling me that he is a painter and adjuring me, as I love the fine arts, to hire or buy him a cow to paint from.'

One joy his royalties brought him : that he was able to increase his help to his two unmarried sisters, Fanny and Selina, who had long been in part dependent on him, and were now living at Brighton where he frequently visited them. Another was the setting up of a brougham of his own. It seemed only fair, as he noted, that he should have some personal advantage from the success of his labours. On 16 January 1851 – four months before the pageant of the great Hyde Park Exhibition began – the brougham arrived, and its owner drove in it to dine at Lord John Russell's, 'pleased and proud, and thinking how unjustly poor Pepys was abused for noting in his diary the satisfaction it gave him to ride in his own coach'.

The pride in his fame and brougham was surpassed a year later by a crowning glory. Since the loss of his seat in 1847 Macaulay had received the offer of several constituencies and, on Palmerston's ejection from the Cabinet in 1851, of a place in the Government. But all such offers he had steadily refused: he had his task. His return to Parliament was finally accomplished in the most remarkable way. In the summer of 1852 his former constituents decided to make amends for the slight they had given him five years before. Nor could all the discouragements they received from the illustrious man whom they had resolved to honour deflect them from their purpose. Macaulay would neither visit them nor give any pledges or even an opinion upon political matters. The only concession he would make them was to intimate that if they chose to elect him on such terms – 'in a manner so honourable and peculiar', as he put it – he would not feel justified in refusing the trust. They did so, and by a handsome majority. Never had Burke's plea for the freedom of parliamentary representatives received so sweeping a vindication.

6

The Finished Man

'An honest man's the noblest work of God.'
(Pope.)

DURING the years in which the great *History* was going
forward, its author was recording the events and thoughts
of every day in his journal. He had begun the practice on
his return from India, describing his visit to France and
Italy in 1837 in a formidable folio volume purchased from
Mr Fell, the stationer in Piccadilly. Thereafter, on his
accession to Cabinet rank, he had abandoned it for close on
ten years, resuming it a few weeks before the publication
of the first part of his *History* in 1848. From that time until
his death he seldom failed to bring it up to date each night.
The bold sloping hand of his entries, so impetuous that at
times it is almost illegible, fills eleven volumes, ranging
in size from the great folio with its seven hundred pages
in which he recorded his last three years of life to the little
paper-cover pocket-books which he took on his continental
holidays.

These journals have never been published, though they
were used with fine judgement by Sir George Trevelyan.
Today they rest in the library of Trinity College, Cambridge, where they were placed by his great-nephew and
fellow historian, the late G. M. Trevelyan. Those who
seek in them such horrid revelations as wink through the
discreet shorthand of that other and greater diary a few
hundred yards distant in the Pepysian library will be
disappointed. Here are no revelations – only an occasional

79

erasion of some more than usually strong expression of the author's dislikes – and after one of these the unexpected and unanswerable comment : 'How my hieroglyphics will trouble any prying person!' Yet in their crowded pages may be found the essence of a great Englishman.

Like all good diarists, Macaulay was doubly interested in the world about him and in himself. He tells us everything : how his stomach was disordered after mixing his wines too freely at the Greenwich 'Trafalgar'; or how he tore his trousers at the knee, falling over the step by Newton's statue as he came out of Trinity Chapel. The passion for detailed narrative which makes the *History* so readable is here also. And the knowledge that he was writing for no eyes but his own begets a certain easy directness of phrasing which is more akin to the spoken than the written word and reminds one of Johnson's table-talk. So he speaks of his contemporaries and their doings : Derby, unable to persuade the Peelites to join his government in 1858, 'means to march the old ragged regiment through Coventry'; Palmerston 'is not the man to decline anything—he would accept the Rectorship of a College in Greenland and be off by the next whaler'; Wilberforce 'used to sing after dinner and so did Brougham, but the fashion is gone out of England'. The same informality, as of one taking his ease in Zion – the quality above all others which is so lacking in the *Essays* – gives a piquancy to every page of Macaulay's diary. Baba, he records one June day in 1853, has told him that a cousin had called his *History* a nasty romance, 'and I said that I would put him down in my journal as a stupid beast, which I do'.

Here is the minute record of a Victorian's daily life. We see him working in the early hours in the quiet of the Albany, with his table covered with the accumulated litter of years – once he was forced to his great benefit to spend

a whole day tidying in order to unearth a long-borrowed
book whose owner had demanded its return – reading
Cicero or the latest novel at breakfast, and then walking
round to Brooks's or the Athenæum to hear the news or
talk like Johnson for victory. Thence he would make his
way Bloomsburywards to his day's labours in the Museum.
But most he liked to visit Hannah and the Trevelyan
children at Clapham or Westbourne Terrace – to chat for
ten minutes stolen from the working hours of morning
with the two dear girls, or spend in their company an
afternoon of 'content, peace and quietness'. He never
grew out of his family, and, when his father's fireside was
no more, clung as eagerly to his sister's. Here all his
feast-days were passed – the Christmas entry is almost
unvarying : 'We had the old dinner—the cod, oysters,
turkey were excellent : then the snapdragon, and the salt
and the laugh—and by that time dear little Alice had been
quite as much excited as her singularly delicate frame will
bear.' He could scarcely record an hour passed with these
loved ones without adding some grateful comment : 'What
a good happy family, fine understandings, sweet tempers,
warm affections, high principles'; and, when the children
grew older, he poured guineas in almost embarrassing
profusion into their hands on their birthdays; 'a small
present', he wrote on one such, 'compared with what I
owe her for twenty-one years of love and kindness'.

Though Macaulay adored children he was at one with
his generation in liking to see them in their right place.
In one house where he dined the children, contrary to the
general rule, were allowed to appear at the dinner-table
and indulge in behaviour at which his indignation knew no
bounds : 'eating of everything at the side tables, squeezing
themselves between the guests', and even climbing up
behind his chair to eat soup out of their mother's spoon :

'an odious nuisance never seen at any house but this'. And towards the youthful failings of his nephew George he could at times be, though always a kind, a very severe critic. Perhaps on the whole he preferred little girls to little boys, and when they grew somewhat older the preference still remained. To a gay, laughing, prattling miss, provided she was tolerably good-looking, he was always glad to unbend; at dinner parties he was a great favourite with the young ladies. Only he liked their beauty to endure : 'Alas! alas!' he notes on meeting an old acquaintance after many years, 'that everything beautiful must fade. How beautiful once!' And when at a friend's house an all-too-ripe widow cast her net at him he fled, confessing that he might have acted otherwise when both were younger : 'before I had grey hairs and she mustachios'.

Though with all the chivalry of his age towards women – he once made a vow never to review the books they wrote lest he should be forced to criticize them – he found it hard to hide his disgust when they fell short of his ideal of their sex. Blue-stockings of any kind he particularly abhorred. Of an acquaintance at a foreign hotel who presented him to his wife, he wrote in his journal : 'He prepared me for the interview by saying that that she was a very great invalid and a great politician, and if he had added to this not very alluring catalogue of female charms that she was exceedingly ugly and disagreeable, he would not have been far wrong.' Nor did he like any infringement of his conceptions of propriety. He was shocked by the dancing of the gallopade at a Christmas ball at Woburn – as voluptuous as the fandango he thought it – and was much distressed at a dinner party by a lady who 'kept on very nearly trespassing beyond the limits of decorum'. On the whole he probably did well to remain a bachelor.

Except for his sister and his nieces, his closest intimates

were all men. At the famous breakfast parties which he and his friends – Hallam the historian, Monckton Milnes, Bishop Wilberforce and Lord Mahon – used to give, he would pour out that amazing talk of which no instance remains, because, as Tom Moore said, to record it one would have needed as wonderful a memory as his own. It was more soliloquy than conversation, irritating to those who wanted to shine themselves but to those humbler ones who preferred to listen delightful beyond expression. 'The only great conversationalist I ever knew', was the Duke of Argyll's testimony. And when anyone interposed a doubt or question, the quick 'Oh, don't you remember?' would introduce some example of that marvellous and all-embracing memory. Macaulay once remarked that any fool could say his Archbishops of Canterbury backwards, and proceeded to do so till someone stopped him at Cranmer. He used to boast that if every copy of *Paradise Lost* and *Paradise Regained* were destroyed he could replace them out of his own head.

Chief among his friends was the lawyer Thomas Flower Ellis. After the latter had lost his wife, the two became inseparable – dining together almost nightly on such noble fare as broiled mackerel, young duck, asparagus, and plovers' eggs at Macaulay's favourite tavern, the 'Trafalgar' at Greenwich, or in his rooms in the Albany. For Ellis's company the great historian more and more eschewed parties and social functions – 'racketing', as he called it – preferring to spend long fire-lit evenings with him discussing Greek authors or laughing at the ludicrous, though somewhat Decameronish, verses which Ellis wrote for their joint amusement. Once, when the two old friends were sitting thus together, Macaulay fell asleep over the fire, but continued talking so coherently that the other for some time noticed no difference.

Often the two would take their holidays together – at Malvern or the Isle of Wight or their favourite Paris. 'By the by,' Macaulay wrote to Ellis in September 1849, when the first-fruits of his *History* were beginning to flow into his pockets, 'you know our contract. I promised to treat you. I do not mean that I will pay for your tubs and towels. But I insist that I order all the dinners and settle the bills. I will give you a round of restaurateurs – Very, the Frères Provenceaux, the Café de Paris, Véfour – and when we have tried them all, we will stick to the best. If you have any scruples about going through this course of experimental gastronomy at the expense of a Plutus like me – a fellow rolling in wealth and about to receive six thousand pounds in a few weeks – I will promise to let you take me to Rome in your carriage and at your own proper charge the first summer after you are a Judge of the Common Pleas.' Very pleasant travels they were that these friends took together : 'I had good health, generally good weather, a good friend and a good servant', is the grateful entry on their return from one such.

Sometimes in term-time, when Ellis could not accompany him, Macaulay took his holidays alone. He was always glad of an opportunity – a burst pipe in his chambers or the coming of the painters – to steal away for a few days to Bristol or the Wye or Brighton, where he would stay at the Norfolk, recalling how in the less decorous days of his youth the Austrian Foreign Minister had cuckolded an English Lord Chancellor there, but adding that since there were now Bibles in all the bedrooms he hoped the pollution had been expiated. On such solitary holidays he would occupy himself in long walks, striding for sixteen miles along the dusty roads round Ventnor with only a single stop for a draught of porter, or slipping away with a volume of Plautus in his pocket to the thickets under Bonchurch to read away a drowsy summer's day.

If books are companions, Macaulay was never alone. He read incessantly – at breakfast, in a carriage crossing the Alps, as he walked the London streets or the Malvern hills. 'What a blessing it is', he once wrote, 'to love books as I love them—to be able to converse with the dead and to live amidst the unreal.' He loved them so much that he was ready to read them all, good or bad, and in the daily entries of his reading there is scarcely one which does not include some reference to his progress in some long and ponderous Victorian novel: 'I do not know why I read such trash', he often adds. Though he thought little of the work of his contemporaries, he occasionally stumbled on something that pleased him: once, almost against his will, he found himself following with laughter the adventures of a certain Soapey Sponge, galloping homerically across the green English shires. Yet the books he loved most were always the books he knew best – the good companions to which he returned again and again. The least tampering with their sacred writ aroused his indignation: when Dr Warburton suggests as an emendation to his favourite *Lear* – 'the finest of all human performances' – the substitution of '*candent* tears' for '*cadent*', Macaulay's marginal comment is 'More fool Warburton.' And where Johnson had softened Hamlet's '*grunt and sweat*' to '*groan and sweat*', on the grounds that modern ears could scarcely bear such language, he wrote across the page: 'We want Shakespeare, not your fine modern English.'

Most of all he returned again and again to the classics. In little more than a year he read all Cicero twice, Plautus three times, and Demosthenes four. Cicero he knew as few of even the greatest scholars have done, following his moral fall and the growth of that all-corroding egotism with profound pity and understanding. He used to say that the pleasure a man took in Cicero was the standard by which his intellectual culture must be measured, and he once got his nephew George into a rare trouble by advising him to read him during a mathematical lecture at Cambridge. Plato he followed in a vast early seventeenth-century folio, a purchase of his youth, measuring sixteen by ten inches and weighing twelve pounds. Often in its crowded margins he seems to be taking part himself in the Socratic dialogue. 'There you are in the Sophist's net', he interposes; 'I think that if I had been in the place of Polus, Socrates would hardly have had so easy a job of it.' And profoundly as he admired that wonderful mind he shared all the irritation that the philosopher's contemporaries must have felt at his personality. 'I do not wonder that they poisoned him', he wrote, 'a pest of a fellow—his delight in humbling everybody else, his mock humility, his quaker-like patience, more provoking than any insolence, would have driven me mad.'

But his strong and acute enjoyment of literature arose mainly from his capacity for appreciation and not from any analytical faculty. The dissecting kind of criticism was beyond him. For this reason his first allegiance was still given, as in the far days of Barley Wood, to the poets – to the great Greek tragedians, to Shakespeare, to Milton, to Dante, above all to Homer. He did not need to read these; he remembered them. Crossing to Ireland, with a fresh breeze and the sun sinking in glory, and the starlight 'like the starlight of the Trades', he found an excellent substitute for reading, going through *Paradise Lost* in his head.

Over the realm of English letters in the prosperous fifties Macaulay reigned supreme. Others in the front rank there were – Dickens, Thackeray, Tennyson – but these were mere novelists and poets, and therefore to the British public altogether on a lower and lighter plane to that of the author of the *History of England* and one who had been in his time a Cabinet Minister and a member of the Supreme Council of India. No man of letters in this country has ever held quite Macaulay's position. Preside over his fellow writers, in the sense that Johnson or Dryden did, he certainly did not: he had too little liking for literary society for that. 'I met Sir Bulwer Lytton or Lytton Bulwer', he once mentions : 'he is anxious for some scheme for some association of literary men. I hate the notion of gregarious authors. The less we have to do with each other the better.' Yet for all that he regarded himself as their representative and the custodian of their good name. When the Queen asked him what he thought about a book of Froude's he spoke of it more highly than he felt it merited, 'not wishing,' he explains, 'to lower him or his work in the estimation of his sovereign.' By his fellow authors of the humbler kind he was literally bombarded with manuscripts which they wanted him to read and, of course, praise : in this they were frequently disappointed, though if they were hard up they could generally count on receiving a cheque by return. But woe betide them if they claimed to pretensions which Macaulay thought unmannerly or arrogant. 'A fool who lives at Ramsgate', he writes of one such, 'has sent me a ranting Socialist and Chartist essay, begging that I will get it published, and telling me that he applies to me because I am the Incarnation of his principles. I will send him an answer that he shall remember to the latest day that he lives.'

Fools of any kind he did not bear kindly. Those who bored him and those who kept him waiting particularly raised his ire. At the board meetings of the British Museum, on which he served as the living representative of letters, he frequently encountered both. 'To the

Museum,' he records : 'long stupid sitting – the Duke of—
a fool, and I little better for going to a place where two
hours are spent in doing what a man of sense and vigour
would despatch in five minutes.' A few months later there
is a change, but only, it transpires, from the frying-pan
into the fire : 'The Duke of —'s death has relieved us of a
great bore. But we have chosen to afflict ourselves with
another, who is as great a fool as his Royal Highness and
has the additional fault of thinking himself a wit – Lord
N—. A sillier, shallower twaddler I never knew. I have
greater difficulty in keeping my temper with him than
with any man with whom I ever did business.' But just
when the enraged historian felt he could bear it no longer,
and was contemplating resignation, death again inter-
vened and he was able to apostrophize : 'Poor Lord N.!
God rest him. But a greater bore I never knew.' When
Macaulay himself took the chair at the Board's meetings,
business went on fast.

It was not only fools whom he did not suffer gladly.
For some of the more eminent of his fellow writers he felt
a strong aversion. The aged author of the *Excursion* he
dismissed briefly as 'a humbug, a bore and a rat', and
added the opinion that the sooner his influence on literature
ceased to be felt the better. Of a younger poet he wrote :
'*Aurora Leigh* is trash—unredeemed trash—bad philosophy,
bad style, bad versification, gross and sometimes indecent
imagery.' And when he sat next to Mrs Gaskell, then
world-famous as the author of *Cranford*, he merely set her
down as 'the writer of a book which I have not read and
am not likely to read'; and even his spelling deserted him
in his scorn at the genus blue-stocking, for he endowed
her name with an i. Particularly did he dislike his fellow
historians. He once was forced to take Miss Strickland in
to dinner : 'Never in my life', he records, 'was I more

disagreeably seated'; and he could never be brought to admit that Carlyle ever penned a sentence that was not meaningless gibberish. 'Carlyle is here undergoing a water cure,' he wrote from Clifton. "I have not seen him yet. But his water-doctor said to S. the other day: "You wonder at his eccentric opinions and style. It is all stomach. I shall set him to rights. He will go away quite a different person." If he goes away writing commonsense and good English, I shall declare myself a convert to Hydropathy.'

Sometimes Macaulay's literary estimates were singularly at fault. When *David Copperfield* first came out, he recorded his opinion that it had better have stayed in, and that its author was a played-out mine. Yet though he thought Dickens's style vulgar and flippant, and considered him far beneath his rival Thackeray, he would never speak or write against him – first, as he said, because he had once eaten his salt, secondly, because he was a good man, and thirdly, because he hated slavery as heartily as he did himself. And if he had strong dislikes, he at least knew what he liked and never failed to praise it. 'Admirable—the greatest man since Milton', he notes after re-reading Burke.

To love anything Macaulay had first to understand and grow familiar with it. He liked things to be clear, even in matters of climate; he loathed fogs and what he called 'moist sloppy weather', and his favourite sky was 'a hard Christmas frost with a sun as red as blood'. Certain things, excellent in themselves, he never tolerated because he never understood them. Philosophy was one of them – 'German humbug', he termed it, 'nothing but objectivity, subjectivity and that trash', and he used to say that he would rather have written *John Gilpin* than all the volumes of Fichte, Kant, Schelling, and Hegel together.

'Did I not point out to you the most absurd article on metaphysics in the new edition of the *Encyclopædia Britannica,*' he enquired of Ellis. 'The author is named Mansell. He has now got into a controversy with as great a fool as himself on the highly interesting and important question whether identity can properly be said to be a quality : whether, for example, one of the qualities of Mr. Thomas Flower Ellis be his being the same person as Mr. Thomas Flower Ellis. Mr. Mansell contends strongly for the negative. He says your being the same person as Mr. Thomas Flower Ellis is not one of your qualities, but the ground or subtraction of your qualities. And these vagabonds pronounce it a desecration to call Bacon and Newton philosophers!'

A good hater Macaulay certainly was. Quakers he loathed – 'the dullest, vilest, most absurd of all Christian sects' – and Mr Spurgeon's preaching and Mr Disraeli. When the latter got into a dispute with Croker in the *Quarterly Review,* Macaulay was delighted: 'They are well matched – two of the greatest scamps living – scandals to literature, scandals to politics, never so well employed, as when abusing and exposing each other.' He hated theoretical Tories, and Radicals – 'your busy, impracticable, uncomprising reformers' – and cabbies because they were always late : 'I would make no concession to these fellows, none', he declared when a cab strike was threatened. He also detested collections in church, which he noted never failed to coincide with his rare attendances. 'A collection as usual', he records. 'I doubted about my giving anything as the charity is one to which I subscribe annually, and it is rather contrary to principle to let a preacher get out of me more than the usual consideration I think appropriate to this purpose. However, I gave something.' And more than all things he hated baseness and dishonesty in any form.

Yet if Macaulay was a good hater, he was also a good lover. He loved the progress that contributed to man's material well-being – the steam engine, the steam carriage, the electric telegraph, the gas-light. He liked to see the common people about him happy : it was characteristic that he delighted in the seventh 'Idyll' of Theocritus, because it was full of 'rural plenty and comfort – flowers, fruit, leaves, fountains, soft goatskins, old wine, singing-birds, joyous friendly companions'. He loved his friends, and was almost absurdly loyal to them where once he had given his heart. He would sometimes, in the case of a very old and trusted companion, even defer his judgement to his, and when at the Manchester Art Gallery he was much struck by Etty's 'Sirens', he was careful to add to this expression of opinion, 'Whether this be good or bad art, God knows! I will ask Lord Lansdowne.'

Above all he loved liberty and he loved his country. It was scarcely wonderful that he loved the former, bred as he was among the men who had slain the slave trade and the slave owner. The hours spent at the feet of the great Greek and Latin republican writers had helped to foster that love. In his writing, as on the floor of the Commons, Macaulay was ever the asserter of the public liberties against kings and arrogant patricians and corrupt administrators, blending ancient and modern thought in so wonderful a way that for a moment Roman plebeian and Victorian Whig seemed one. So he marched proudly in the van of the Whig crusade for liberty with John Russell and his kin :

> the good house
> That loved the people well.

Only by the time he reached their lines the foes he had come to slay were no more : the Tory despots had all vanished. Yet when new enemies to freedom arose, threatening to bind the future as they had the past, the vigilant old champion was ready to cross swords with them : the joint-stock capitalist, Railway Hudson – 'Mammon and Belial rolled into one' – or the all-destroying tyranny of an absolute democracy, then in its first infancy, in which he saw infinite possibilities of future peril. In the last years of his life he wrote a remarkable letter to an American friend confiding these fears :

I have long been convinced that institutions purely democratic must, sooner or later, destroy liberty or civilisation, or both. In Europe, where the population is dense, the effect of such institutions would be almost instantaneous. What happened lately in France is an example. In 1848 a pure democracy was established there. During a short time there was reason to expect a general spoliation, a national bankruptcy, a new partition of the soil, a maximum of prices, a ruinous load of taxation laid on the rich for the purpose of supporting the poor in idleness.

Such a system would, in twenty years, have made France as poor and barbarous as the France of the Carlovingians. Happily, the danger was averted ; and now there is a despotism, a silent tribune, an enslaved press. Liberty is gone, but civilisation has been saved.

I have not the smallest doubt that if we had a purely democratic Government here the effect would be the same. Either the poor would plunder the rich, and civilisation would perish ; or order and prosperity would be saved by a strong military government and liberty would perish. You may think that your country enjoys an exemption from these evils. I will frankly own to you that I am of a very different opinion. Your fate I believe to be certain, though it is deferred by a physical cause. As long as you have a boundless extent of fertile and unoccupied land, your labouring population will be far more at ease than the labouring population of the Old World, and, while that is the case, the Jeffersonian policy may continue to exist without causing any fatal calamity. But the time will come when New England will be as thickly peopled as Old England. Wages will be as low and will fluctuate as much with you as with us. You will have your Manchesters and your Birminghams, and in those Manchesters and Birminghams hundreds of thousands of artisans will assuredly be sometimes out of work. Then your institutions will be fairly brought to the test. Distress everywhere makes the labourer mutinous and discontented and inclines him to listen with eagerness to agitators, who tell him that it is monstrous iniquity that one man should have a million while another man cannot get a full meal. . . . It is quite plain that your Government will never be able to restrain a distressed and discontented majority. For with you the majority is the Government and has the rich, who are always a minority, absolutely at its mercy. The day will come when in the State of New York a multitude of people, not one of whom has had more than half a breakfast or expects to have more than half a dinner, will choose a legislature. Is it possible to doubt what sort of a legislature will be chosen? On one side is a statesman preaching patience, respect for vested rights, strict observance of public faith. On the other is a demagogue ranting about the tyranny of capitalists and usurers, and asking why anybody should be permitted to drink champagne and to ride in a carriage while thousands of honest folks are in want of necessaries. Which of the two candidates is likely to be preferred by a working-man who hears his children crying for more bread? I seriously apprehend that you will, in some such season of adversity as I have described, do things which will prevent prosperity from returning; that you will act like a people who should in a year of scarcity devour all the seedcorn, and thus make the next a year not of scarcity, but of absolute famine. There will be, I fear, spoliation. The spoliation will increase the distress. The distress will produce fresh spoliation. There is nothing to stop you. Your Constitution is all sail and no anchor. As I said before, when a society has entered on its downward progress, either civilisation or liberty must perish. Either some Caesar or Napoleon will seize the reins of Government, with a strong hand, or your Republic will be as fearfully plundered and laid waste by barbarians in the twentieth century as the Roman Empire was in the fifth; with this difference, that the Huns and Vandals who ravaged the Roman Empire came from without, and that your Huns and Vandals will have been engendered within your own country by your own institutions.

Strongest of all was Macaulay's love for his country. 'England is so great', he wrote of an Irish book full of hatred against her, 'that an Englishman cares little what others think of her or how they talk of her.' For the foreigner and his doings, as for everything he could not understand, he had a magnificent scorn. 'I have found here and there', he remarks of the first frail bud of continental sanitation, 'an attempt at a water-closet, but always an unsuccessful attempt.' And when in Rome an insolent cabman followed him into his hotel demanding a higher fare he flung him into the street with his own hands. 'I do not know how it is,' he added that night in his diary, 'but I have been in three brawls to-day and all with low people.' Every achievement of England's filled him with pride, and when he travelled outside her borders it was with the manifest consciousness that he was a citizen of no mean city. Once on one of his holidays in France he encountered a band of English navvies employed, at a time when English workmanship was the envy of the world, on the construction of a railway. He sent for them and begged them to let a fellow-countryman treat them to breakfast, giving them a napoleon for the purpose. So a citizen of imperial Rome in a distant land saluted the Eagles. 'I am anxious', he wrote in the dark days of 1854, 'about our brave fellows in the Crimea, but proud for the country, and glad to think that the national spirit is so high and unconquerable.'

His vaunted Liberalism had indeed far more in common
with the proud Whigs who threw down the gauntlet to
Louis XIV and whose historian he was than with the
Manchester pacifists of his own day. He was no senti-
mentalist or craven in his politics. 'You call me a Liberal,'
he once said, 'but I don't know that in these days I deserve
the name. I am opposed to the abolition of standing armies.
I am opposed to the abrogation of capital punishment. I am
opposed to the destruction of the National Church. In
short, I am in favour of war, hanging, and Church
Establishments!'

With such tenets Macaulay had a natural leaning towards
Lord Palmerston, whom, indeed, he much admired. 'I
rejoice in his luck most sincerely,' he wrote after one of
that statesman's remarkable feats of extrication from an
awkward scrape, 'for, though he now and then trips, he is
an excellent Minister, and I cannot bear the thought of his
being a sacrifice to the spite of foreign powers.' When
asked to take office after Palmerston's dismissal he refused
to do so, and at the end of a Latin poem of his nephew's he
added lines commemorating the awe in which the great
Foreign Secretary's name was held throughout the world.
Chosen leader and writer of their countrymen in the
fighting fifties, the two veterans pass before us – erect, top-
hatted, confident of mien and with something irrepressibly
English in every poise of their bodies.

Macaulay's nephew has left us a picture of the sturdy
old dictator of mid-Victorian letters as he appeared in these
years – 'sitting bolt upright, his hands resting on the arm
of his chair or folded over the handle of his walking stick,
knitting his great eyebrows as if the subject was one which
had to be thought out as he went along, or brightening
from the forehead downwards when a burst of humour was
coming.' Less conventional but as illuminating is the

description of a New York journalist, as retailed by the sitter himself in a letter to Margaret Trevelyan:

> The writer says that I am a stout man with hazel eyes; that I always walk with an umbrella; that I sometimes bang the umbrella against the ground; that I often dine in the Coffee room of the *Trafalgar* on fish; that once he saw me break a decanter there, but that I did not appear to be at all ashamed of my awkwardness, but called for my bill as coolly as if nothing had happened.

When Macaulay saw the portrait of himself which Richmond painted in 1850 he was not displeased – the face of a man, he noted, of considerable mental powers, great boldness and frankness, and a quick relish for pleasure. It reminded him of Mr Fox's.

Far down beneath that downright exterior lay the springs of poetry. 'I saw the lights of Dublin Bay', he writes after a voyage. 'I love entering a port at night – the contrast between the wild lonely sea and the life and turmoil of a harbour when a ship is coming in.' To Matthew Arnold Macaulay seemed only the giant embodiment of the English middle-class Philistine, terrible as an army with banners and smashing down all beauty in his path. Yet his writing is full of passages in which some intense depth of feeling seems to well over: that, for instance, in which he pictures Bunyan at work on his *Pilgrim's Progress*:

> Images came crowding on his mind faster than he could put them into words, quagmires and pits, steep hills, dark and horrible glens, soft vales, sunny pastures, a gloomy castle of which the courtyard was strewn with the skulls and bones of murdered prisoners, a town all bustle and splendour, like London on the Lord Mayor's Day, and the narrow path, straight as a rule could make it, running on up hill and down hill,

through city and through wilderness, to the Black River and the Shining Gate.

As for his religion, it is difficult to set any exact name to it. He had travelled a long road from the strict observances and narrow views of his father's sect. Religious persecution of any kind he loathed with all his soul, and when a delegation of fervent fellow parishioners begged him to draw up a scathing denunciation of a measure extending some small favour to Catholics, he treated them to a speech which he reckoned they would remember to their dying days. He seldom went to church, and when he did it was only to record afterwards his almost unvarying disapproval of the sermon – 'a bad sermon as usual', 'a most detestable sermon', and the best he could be brought to was a grudging 'a middling sermon'. Yet he was strict in his own life, full of compassion for suffering wherever he recognized it and generous in charity to a fault. Once in a marginal note to a theological work, he came near to defining his creed. 'If', ran the text, 'to live strictly and think freely; to practise what is moral and to believe what is rational, be consistent with the profession of Christianity, then I shall acquit myself like one of its truest professors.' Here, Macaulay wrote, was truth : *'haec est absoluta et perfecta philosophi vita'*.

7

Into the Shadows

He felt that his time was short, and grieved, with a
grief such as only noble spirits feel, to think that he
must leave his work but half finished.
(Macaulay, *History*.)

On 25 October 1850, Macaulay wrote in his journal:

My birthday. I am fifty. Well, I have had a happy life. I do
not know that anybody, whom I have seen close, has had a
happier. Some things I regret: but, on the whole, who is better
off? I have not children of my own, it is true; but I have
children whom I love as if they were my own, and who, I
believe, love me. I wish that the next ten years may be as happy
as the last ten. But I rather wish it than hope it.

The first signs of change, which even he, who hated
change so much, could not hide from himself were at hand.
For a long time he had been troubled by mysterious attacks
of giddiness and a recurrent tendency to bleed in the head;
and though the time had been when north-east and south-
west wind were all one to him they were so no more. He
would wince for a moment: then, recalling his compensa-
tions, return to his labours. But in the summer that saw
his triumph at Edinburgh there came a foreboding of
something more ominous, which crept even into his
working hours: he scarcely knew what. Days passed when
he could not write at all; only by struggling fiercely with
himself could he shake off a feeling of dullness, never
known to him before, and begin again. Bright, his doctor,
gave him enough calomel, as his victim said, to purge

three bilious elephants, but all to no purpose. 'How I worked a year ago,' he wrote, 'and why cannot I work so now.' On 22 July 1852, nine days after his election, extreme debility, long impending, and a deep pain in his chest warned him that something was radically wrong, and he sent for Bright. The latter found that the action of the heart was seriously deranged. When the curtain rises again on Macaulay it is at Clifton, where Hannah had taken him: walking slowly, lest the palpitations should begin again, across the thunder-dewed August fields. Here he remained all that autumn, talking much of old times and faces and revisiting Barley Wood and the friendly green places of his childhood.

With the need to be still there came to this over-busied spirit an intense and almost painful sense of the world's beauty. The sight of a cart-load of children in a Somerset lane singing and laughing for sheer joy at their ride could make him catch his breath: he had been so long buried in books that he had almost forgotten the earth around him. He knew now that his days on it were numbered: sometimes, when he thought how few they must be, and how soon he must leave those he loved, he could hardly control his tears.

From this time forward Macaulay was an invalid. That winter bronchitis came to him, and thereafter the fogs of each succeeding winter brought with them long-dreaded fits of asthmatic coughing. It was as though a chain had been laid on him: he could walk slowly only and with pain for a few hundred yards before he was forced to return; the hours of work were broken by the need of frequent rest; he was a prisoner. But yield he would not. He knew now he could never reach the end of his task: the ocean of the eighteenth century would not be sailed by him. Yet before he went down towards the shadows he would finish William;

he would not go hence till that was done. So he pleaded ever with Charon for a respite.

To his task once more he committed himself. 'I sat down doggedly to work', ran his oft-repeated phrase, borrowing old Johnson's adverb. Sometimes he felt that he could never accomplish it; that his reputation would sink to nothingness in his own time, leaving him among a generation that would marvel at his former fame. Yet each month of his own life saw another month added to that chronicle of a nation's life which he was telling, and still the flowing pages kept their majestic pace. Something of the fore-knowledge of death entered, too, into his style : from the time of his illness his work is marked by a certain bare and beautiful economy of words, hitherto alien to him. The little articles he wrote in these years for the *Encyclopædia Britannica* – on Atterbury, Bunyan, Goldsmith, and Johnson – are masterpieces of compression.

Nor would he surrender one iota of the life outside his task that he could still retain. Although urged by his doctors to apply for the Chiltern Hundreds, he would not do so. His attendances in the House were rare and he spoke but seldom, yet when he did he was listened to with universal respect, and almost with awe. When in the summer of 1853 he rose after a six years' silence, the sleepy Wednesday Committees adjourned in haste and the lobbies filled with members running towards the chamber with the cry that Macaulay was up. He spoke for forty minutes, in the quiet tones of 'a man of the world, confiding his learning, his recollections, and his logic to a party of gentlemen', and, when he sat down, a private measure which but for his intervention would have passed almost without opposition was rejected by an overwhelming majority. In the same session he spoke on the India Bill – 'one of those bursts of conversation which would have charmed the breakfast or

cheered the dinner-table', as Disraeli from across the
gangway called it – in favour of recruiting the Indian Civil
Service by competitive examination. Later he served as
Chairman of the Committee for putting the new system
into practice, and wrote its Report. But the late nights in
crowded lobby and stifling chamber proved more than his
broken health could bear.

Yet, though forced to abandon his public work and save
his vitality as best he could for his unfinished task, his love
for life was undiminished. So was his courage. When an
epidemic of burglaries alarmed the neighbourhood, he
announced his intention of buying a gun. And when
nervous friends were disturbed by the prospect of the
popular saturnalia to be held in the Green Park on Oak
Apple Day, the old stalwart was full of scorn. In his youth,
like all his generation, he had been nervous of the rough
unpoliced London mob; he was so no more, for he knew
his England too well. He gave his servants leave to watch
the festivities from the top of the house : as for himself, he
said, he would not stir. But when the evening came and
the sounds of the fireworks reached him, he could not
refrain from hobbling to the window of his bedroom to
view the show – 'very beautiful it was', he thought – and
only a sprained leg from which he was suffering prevented
him from joining the gaping servants on the roof. One
showery day in the summer of 1854, while walking in the
water-meadows near Esher, where he was staying with the
Trevelyans, he turned into an ale-house and encountered a
party of poor Surrey hop-pickers, weary after a long tramp
homewards from a fruitless season. They called for beer,
and a foaming pot of ale was set before them but when they
learnt its price, they put it down untasted. Macaulay pulled
out the money and bade them drink. Their simple gratitude
gave him deep pleasure; he left them, he recorded in his

journal, followed by more blessings than he believed were ever before purchased for ninepence.

That summer at Esher saw him often at Hampton Court, pursuing his work beneath the trees of his hero, William's, palace. Despite his infirmities, seldom a week passed without his completing seven or eight pages. When winter came he was back at the Albany, buried in pamphlets and broadsides, and turning away, as he put it, from the miseries of Balaclava and the Crimea to the battle of Steinkirk. Consciousness of the magnitude of his labours and the shortness of his time made him impatient to be done : he had reached a point at which he was glad when he learnt that there was no more to be discovered. By November 1855 he was once more correcting proofs. A month later the second part of his *History*, bringing his tale to 1691, was published.

Its success surpassed even that of the first part. Twenty-five thousand copies of the two volumes were struck off, yet before the day of publication Longmans wrote to tell him that they had been compelled to print a further five thousand. No such edition of a work of that magnitude had ever been known before. To its author its triumph spelt wealth and such fame as even he had not yet known. Yet his heart was still that of a child, and turning again to his Thucydides he prayed that neither age nor riches would harden him.

Macaulay's achievement was little short of miraculous. He succeeded in making history the favourite reading of the general public of his day. In a single year fourteen thousand copies of one volume were sold in the United Kingdom alone : and in a generation a hundred and forty thousand copies of the entire *History*. In America its sale was even vaster – a fact which much puzzled its author, for, as he observed, the book was entirely insular in spirit. It was translated into almost every language, even Persian, and Macaulay was honoured by the acclamations of the learned academies of every part of the world. He was even made that which in his youth he had pretended to guard his pockets against in a crowd – a German knight!

Wealth his triumph brought in almost as great a measure as fame. Even before the appearance of the second part, the steadily accumulating sale of the earlier volumes had raised his income to close on £4,000 a year : like Dogberry, he told his friends, he would soon have two gowns and everything handsome about him. Three months after the publication of part two, Longmans, anticipating the time for payment, sent him a cheque for £20,000. The thought of being so opulent gave him much amusement. It tickled his fancy to sit in the parlour of his old friend Henry Thornton, the banker, in Birchin Lane and discuss with him the ways and means of investment. 'I think,' he remarked, as Thornton explained the various classes of Spanish government stock, 'I catch your meaning. Active Spanish Bonds profess to pay interest now, and do not. Deferred Spanish Bonds profess to pay interest at some future time, and will not. Passive Spanish Bonds profess to pay interest neither now nor at any future time! I think you might buy a large amount of Passive Spanish Bonds for a very small sum!' He could make his friends comfortable now with a clear conscience. The wealth was all the greater because it was his practice to pay all bills within twenty-four hours and to treat his literary gains as capital. Anything over he gave away, and with both hands.

In 1856 there came two changes in his life. In January he bade farewell to his constituents and, nearly thirty-six years after he first entered it, quitted the House of Commons. Spring saw a further alteration. For some time he had been looking for an acre of green turf where, as he told an American friend, he could be within reach of his

Clubs and the Museum, yet out of the reach of the coal fogs and rain fogs which for six months in the year made it so hard for him to breathe. On 1 May he entertained Ellis for the last time in his rooms in the Albany, and the next day moved into a pleasant house which he had bought for himself in a wooded lane on Campden Hill. Here at Holly Lodge he could step from his library windows on to a green lawn, and here turn gardener, rejoicing in the rhododendrons and laburnums that grew round his little fountain, or rooting out the 'impudent flaring, yellow faces' of the dandelions with as fierce a joy as ever he fell upon the Tories. He was happier here; sleep came more easily and refreshingly; and near at hand were Hannah and the Trevelyan children in Westbourne Terrace, whom he still loved to entertain on feast days in traditional style – to a goose on Michaelmas Day, and oysters and a mighty turkey at Christmas. After the sixth dozen, he used to tell his young guests, oysters cease to whet the appetite.

Here nearly all Macaulay's remaining days were passed. The Argyll children next door loved to watch the great historian walking up and down his verandah with his book in his hand, occasionally diving out to destroy a weed or a slug. Sometimes he would tear himself away from his little paradise of turf and shrubs to accompany the Trevelyans on some holiday ramble, crossing the Alps to see Venice for the first time or sampling the English Lakes, where he laughingly suggested that he should turn an honest penny by charging the trippers for the treat of seeing him stand by Wordsworth's grave at Grasmere. And sometimes also he would visit old friends – Lord Lansdowne at Bowood or the Stanhopes at Chevening, where he would watch his little Valentine, Lady Mary, dancing among the flowers. But all too often when he went abroad he was forced indoors wheezing by the fire and longing to be back by his own hearth. He drew his breath more freely there.

On 28 August 1857, Macaulay, as he was seated at dinner at Holly Lodge, received news of an honour all the more gratifying on account of the source from which it emanated. 'I had hardly begun to eat,' he wrote in his journal, 'when a message came with a letter from Palmerston. An offer of a peerage : the Queen's pleasure already taken. I was very much surprised. Perhaps no such offer was ever made without the slightest solicitation, direct or indirect, to a man of humble origin and moderate fortune who had long quitted public life.' He had no scruples about accepting, which he did gratefully, taking the title of Lord Macaulay of Rothley after his birthplace. Henceforward, he told his nieces, they must be careful to address him in the manner of the seventeenth century as 'Right Honourable my Singular Good Lord'! In the same autumn he was unanimously elected High Steward of the Borough of Cambridge. It pleased him to be associated with his old University town and with an office that had been held in its time by Bacon, Cromwell and Clarendon.

Far dearer to Macaulay than any worldly honours were his books. When the lamps were lit and his day's work laid aside his house was peopled by hundreds of friendly shadows more solid to him than any reality. Some were of his own native English breed : Parson Adams would sit beside him at his pipe, or Elizabeth Bennet peer round the door, and the silver of Mr Valiant-for-Truth's armour glint across the moonlit lawn between the parting of the curtains. But most of all the old scholar loved to have about him, when the London fogs shrouded the city below, the spirits of men bred in a clearer clime whom he had loved since his earliest youth. Sometimes as he turned the pages he could not restrain his tears – 'crying for Achilles cutting off his hair, crying for Priam rolling on the ground in the courtyard of his house; mere imaginary beings, creatures of an old ballad-maker who died three thousand years ago.'

For other and newer writers he had little love. The lower lip would project and the great brow darken above his contracting eyes in outward expression of that intense and unshakeable conservatism. He had never liked changes in the things he knew, and, as he grew older, he liked it less and less. New men, new modes, what were they to him? Pre-Raphaelitism, perish all such affections, and, as for the nerveless, milk-and-water set of young fellows in the House of Commons, the old senator despised them with all his heart. Perhaps he was angriest of all with those who dared to criticize his *History* : a pedantic lawyer, called Paget, kept fastening on to certain of his bold statements and facts in the most insolent way. He would not answer his spiteful trash, not he : no man, the old Whig Bentley had said, could ever be written down but by himself. Posterity would read what he wrote; his critics if he but ignored them would soon be forgotten.

The petulance which he sometimes permitted himself in his dealings with the outside world was never shown to those he loved. To such as were dependent on him – to his servants, to his relations – he was unfailingly gentle and kind. In the early summer of 1858 he paid a visit to his nephew at Cambridge, entertaining a party of under-graduates with his wonderful talk at breakfast and then tottering across Clare Bridge and along the edge of the lawn of King's. It was painfully obvious how weak he was growing with age : but he struggled hard to conceal it. 'I begin to sit loose to life', he wrote. He knew that the last scene of the play was approaching : he would meet it, he resolved, with fortitude and gentleness. Only it saddened him, as he wrote of his own William, 'with a grief such as only noble spirits feel, to think that he must leave his work but half finished'.

Bravely he struggled with it. His frame was broken by a perpetual cough, and the tendency to indolence was stronger and more frequent than before. 'How the days steal away,' he recorded; 'I think often of Johnson's lamentations repeated every Easter over his own idleness.' Yet he would comfort himself by recalling how often before he had desponded and laboured in vain to please himself, yet ended by pleasing the world. In the final months of his life, he wrote some of his finest passages – the description of the Darien fiasco, of the fire at Whitehall, of the recognition of the Old Pretender by Louis. The tragedy was that he was conscious that he was only just beginning to learn how to write, and soon he would be able to write no more.

In October 1859 there came a heavy blow. Trevelyan had left England earlier in the year to take up an appointment as Governor of Madras, and it was now definitely decided that in February Hannah, taking Alice with her, should sail to join him. The parting which Macaulay had dreaded all his life was to come at last, and in little more than three months' time. Profound and overwhelming sorrow oppressed him at the thought of it; he knew it was right and necessary, yet could scarcely bring himself to face it. To hide his grief more than ever he turned to his work, tasking all his slender strength to accomplish it. At least, he resolved, he would see one more volume through the press before he died. By 14 December he had brought his narrative to the end of the session 1699–1700. There the noble edifice stops short on the brink of the eighteenth century it had still to bridge, though two isolated fragments project above the waters beyond – the description of William's death which, himself a dying man, he had sketched in rough manuscript, and the biography of the younger Pitt, which he wrote in the last year of his life for the *Encyclopædia Britannica*.

That December there was an intense frost. The cold, the anguish of that approaching parting, and the strain of overwork combined to produce a heaviness of mind and body almost beyond his bearing. On 19 December he recorded his sensations in his journal:

Still intense frost. I could hardly use my razor for the palpitation of the heart. I feel as if I were twenty years older since last Thursday; – as if I were dying of old age. I am perfectly ready, and shall never be readier. A month more of such days as I have been passing of late would make me impatient to get to my little narrow crib, like a weary factory child.

The doctors examined him but could find no organic affection, only that the heart was a little weak. On 21 December a thaw set in, with heavy rain and great clouds from the south-west driving fast through the sky. That afternoon the sun shone for a few moments and Macaulay ventured out into the garden. Again the doctors were optimistic promising that if his heart would but act with force all his ills would vanish. 'They may be right,' he recorded. 'I am certainly very poorly – weak as a child. Yet' – and almost he hoped – 'I am less nervous than usual. I have shed no tears during some days, though with me tears ask only leave to flow, as poor Cowper says. I am sensible of no intellectual decay; not the smallest.' But two days later he fainted at his work and lay unconscious for many hours. Yet even still the doctors feared no danger.

His sister spent Christmas Day with him. She tried to cheer him, but his emotion at the thought of her approaching voyage to India was so unrestrained that she felt it would be unwise to remain with him too long. He seemed to those who loved him to be lost in an impenetrable mist of unhappiness.

On Wednesday 28 December, the Feast of the Innocents, the old Whig champion roused himself to dictate a letter to a poor curate enclosing a cheque for £25, and signed his name to it. After that he wrote no more. Early in the evening his nephew, George Trevelyan, called at the house, intending to stay to dinner. But his uncle's collapsed appearance and the broken irregularity of his answers caused him to change his mind. There was something radically wrong, he felt, and he hurried home to fetch his mother.

But in the library at Holly Lodge, Macaulay did not move. There was no sound in the room now. Perhaps it was best so. His last days had been cast in a quiet time of England's history, and he had been glad of it, knowing from his studies that it was a sad thing to live in an age of which it was stirring to read. He had been born when England was struggling for her very existence : he had seen her triumph over all her enemies – French sans-culottes, Berlin decrees, Napoleon and the bearskins of the Guard; administrative corruption, financial depression, revolutionary gatherings, Chartist petitions. He had lived to see his country the unchallenged arbiter of the world. And now that his own time of eclipse had come her sun still shone in unbroken glory. Great changes there might be in the womb of time – Italian union, American Civil War, Prussian militarism dominant and victorious, he knew nothing of these. The greatness of England pervaded the whole earth, and he had been her chronicler.

They found him sitting upright in his chair, with a book still open at his side. The heart had stopped, and the historian had become part of that which he had made it his business to record.

Appendices

1. INDIAN EDUCATION : MINUTE OF 2 FEBRUARY 1835

[On his arrival in India, as a Member of the Supreme Council, Macaulay was appointed President of the Committee of Public Instruction, which he found irreconcilably split into two factions : the orientalists and those who wanted to teach the Indians Western learning. He addressed this minute to the Governor General, Lord Bentinck, who, on 7 March, pronounced in favour of 'the promotion of European literature and science among the natives of India'.]

We now come to the gist of the matter. We have a fund to be employed as Government shall direct for the intellectual improvement of the people of this country. The simple question is, what is the most useful way of employing it?

All the parties seem to be agreed on one point, that the dialects commonly spoken among the natives of this part of India, contain neither literary nor scientific information, and are, moreover, so poor and rude that, until they are enriched from some other quarter, it will not be easy to translate any valuable work into them. It seems to be admitted on all sides, that the intellectual improvement of those classes of the people who have the means of pursuing higher studies can at present be effected only by means of some language not vernacular amongst them.

What then shall that language be? One-half of the Committee maintain that it should be the English. The other half strongly recommended the Arabic and Sanscrit. The whole question seems to me to be, which language is the best worth knowing?

I have no knowledge of either Sanscrit or Arabic.—But I have done what I could to form a correct estimate of their value. I have read translations of the most celebrated Arabic and Sanscrit works. I have conversed both here and at home with men distinguished by their proficiency in the Eastern tongues. I am quite ready to take the Oriental learning at the valuation of the Orientalists themselves. I have never found one among them who could deny that a single shelf of a good European library was worth the whole native literature of India and Arabia. The intrinsic superiority of the Western literature is, indeed, fully admitted by those members of the Committee who support the Oriental plan of education.

It will hardly be disputed, I suppose, that the department of literature in which the Eastern writers stand highest is poetry. And I certainly never met with any Orientalist who ventured to maintain that the Arabic and Sanscrit poetry could be compared to that of the great European nations. But when we pass from works of imagination to works in which facts are recorded, and general principles investigated, the superiority of the Europeans becomes absolutely immeasurable. It is, I believe, no exaggeration to say, that all the historical information which has been collected from all the books written in the Sanscrit language is less valuable than what may be found in the most paltry abridgments used at preparatory schools in England. In every branch of physical or moral philosophy, the relative position of the two nations is nearly the same.

How, then, stands the case? We have to educate a people who cannot at present be educated by means of their mother-tongue. We must teach them some foreign language. The claims of our own language it is hardly necessary to recapitulate. It stands pre-eminent even among the languages of the West. It abounds with works of imagination not inferior to the noblest which Greece has bequeathed to us; with models of every species of eloquence; with historical compositions, which, considered as vehicles of ethical and political instruction, have never been equalled; with just and lively representations of human life and human nature; with the most profound speculations on meta-physics, morals, government, jurisprudence, and trade; with full and correct information respecting every experimental science which tends to preserve the health, to increase the comfort, or to expand the intellect of man. Whoever knows that language has ready access to all the vast intellectual wealth, which all the wisest nations of the earth have created and hoarded in the course of ninety generations. It may safely be said, that the literature now extant in that language is of far greater value than all the literature which three hundred years ago was extant in all the languages of the world together. Nor is this all. In India, English is the language spoken by the ruling class. It is spoken by the higher class of natives at the seats of Government. It is likely to become the language of commerce throughout the seas of the East. It is the language of two great European communities which are rising, the one in the south of Africa, the other in Australasia; communities which are every year becoming more important, and more closely connected with our Indian empire. Whether we look at the intrinsic value of our literature, or at the particular situation of this country, we shall see the strongest reason to think that, of all foreign tongues, the English tongue is that which would be the most useful to our native subjects.

The question now before us is simply whether, when it is in our power to teach this language, we shall teach languages in which, by universal confession, there are no books on any subject which deserve to be compared to our own; whether, when we can teach European science, we shall teach systems which, by universal confession, whenever they differ from those of Europe, differ for the worse; and whether, when we can patronise sound Philosophy and true History, we shall countenance, at the public expense, medical doctrines which would disgrace an English farrier,—Astronomy, which would move laughter in girls at an English boarding school,—History, abounding with kings thirty feet high, and reigns thirty thousand years long,—and Geography, made up of seas of treacle and seas of butter.

We are not without experience to guide us. History furnishes several analogous cases, and they all teach the same lesson. There are in modern times, to go no further, two memorable instances of a great impulse given to the mind of a whole society,—of prejudices overthrown,—of knowledge diffused,—

of taste purified,—of arts and sciences planted in countries which had recently been ignorant and barbarous.

The first instance to which I refer, is the great revival of letters among the Western nations at the close of the fifteenth and the beginning of the sixteenth century. At that time almost every thing that was worth reading was contained in the writings of the ancient Greeks and Romans. Had our ancestors acted as the Committee of Public Instruction has hitherto acted; had they neglected the language of Cicero and Tacitus; had they confined their attention to the old dialects of our own island; had they printed nothing and taught nothing at the universities but Chronicles in Anglo-Saxon, and Romances in Norman-French, would England have been what she now is? What the Greek and Latin were to the contemporaries of More and Ascham, our tongue is to the people of India. The literature of England is now more valuable than that of classical antiquity. I doubt whether the Sanscrit literature be as valuable as that of our Saxon and Norman progenitors. In some departments,—in History, for example, I am certain that it is much less so.

Another instance may be said to be still before our eyes. Within the last hundred and twenty years, a nation which has previously been in a state as barbarous as that in which our ancestors were before the crusades, has gradually emerged from the ignorance in which it was sunk, and has taken its place among civilized communities.—I speak of Russia. There is now in that country a large educated class, abounding with persons fit to serve the state in the highest functions, and in no wise inferior to the most accomplished men who adorn the best circles of Paris and London. There is reason to hope that this vast empire, which in the time of our grandfathers was probably behind the Punjab, may, in the time of our grandchildren, be pressing close on France and Britain in the career of improvement. And how was this change effected? Not by flattering national prejudices: not by feeding the mind of the young Muscovite with the old women's stories which his rude fathers had believed: not by filling his head with lying legends about St. Nicholas: not by encouraging him to study the great question, whether the world was or was not created on the 13th of September : not by calling him 'a learned native', when he has mastered all these points of knowledge : but by teaching him those foreign languages in which the greatest mass of information had been laid up, and thus putting all that information within his reach. The languages of Western Europe civilized Russia. I cannot doubt that they will do for the Hindoo what they have done for the Tartar.

2. HISTORY OF ENGLAND: THE BATTLE OF THE BOYNE

When William caught sight of the valley of the Boyne, he could not suppress an exclamation and a gesture of delight. He had been apprehensive that the enemy would avoid a decisive action, and would protract the war till the autumnal rains should return with pestilence in their train. He was now at ease. It was plain that the contest would be sharp and short. The pavilion of James was pitched on the eminence of Donore. The flags of the House of Stuart and of the House of Bourbon waved together in defiance on the walls of Drogheda. All the southern bank of the river was lined by the camp and batteries of the hostile army. Thousands of armed men were moving about among the tents; and every one, horse soldier or foot soldier, French or Irish, had a white badge in his hat. That colour had been chosen in compliment to the House of Bourbon. 'I am glad to see you, gentlemen,' said the King, as his keen eye surveyed the Irish lines. 'If you escape me now, the fault will be mine.'

Each of the contending princes had some advantages over his rival. James, standing on the defensive, behind entrenchments, with a river before him, had the stronger position : but his troops were inferior both in number and in quality to those which were opposed to him. He probably had thirty thousand men. About a third part of this force consisted of excellent French infantry and excellent Irish cavalry. But the rest of his army was the coffs of all Europe. The Irish dragoons were bad; the Irish foot worse. It was said that their ordinary way of fighting was to discharge their pieces once, and then to run away bawling 'Quarter', and 'Murder'. Their inefficiency was, in that age, commonly imputed, both by their enemies and by their allies, to natural poltroonery. How little ground there was for such an imputation has since been signally proved by many brave achievements in every part of the globe. It ought indeed, even in the seventeenth century, to have occurred to reasonable men, that a race which furnished some of the best horse soldiers in the world, would certainly, with judicious training, furnish good foot soldiers. But the Irish foot soldiers had not merely not been well trained : they had been elaborately ill trained. The greatest of our generals repeatedly and emphatically declared that even the admirable army which fought its way, under his command, from Torres Vedras to Toulouse, would, if he had suffered it to contract habits of pillage, have become, in a few weeks, unfit for all military purposes. What then was likely to be the character of troops who, from the day on which they enlisted, were not merely permitted, but invited, to supply the deficiences of pay by marauding ? They were, as might have been expected, a mere mob, furious indeed and clamorous in their zeal for the cause which they had espoused, but incapable of opposing a steadfast resistance to a well ordered force. In truth, all that the discipline, if it is to be so called, of James's army had done for the Celtic kerne had been to debase and enervate him. After eighteen months of nominal soldiership, he was positively farther from being a soldier than on the day on which he quitted his hovel for the camp.

William had under his command near thirty six thousand men, born in many lands, and speaking many tongues. Scarcely one Protestant Church, scarcely one Protestant nation, was unrepresented in the army which a strange series of events had brought to fight for the Protestant religion in the remotest island of the west. About half the troops were natives of England. Ormond was there with the Life Guards, and Oxford with the Blues. Sir John Lanier, an officer who had acquired military experience on the Continent, and whose prudence was held in high esteem, was at the head of the Queen's regiment of horse, now the First Dragoon Guards. There were Beaumont's foot, who had, in defiance of the mandate of James, refused to admit Irish papists among them, and Hastings's foot, who had, on the disastrous day of Killiecrankie, maintained the military reputation of the Saxon race. There were the two Tangier battalions, hitherto known only by deeds of violence and rapine, but destined to begin on the following morning a long career of glory. Two fine English regiments, which had been in the service of the States General, and had often looked death in the face under William's leading, followed him in this campaign, not only as their general, but as their native King. They now rank as the fifth and sixth of the line. The former was led by an officer who had no skill in the higher parts of military science, but whom the whole army allowed to be the bravest of all the brave, John Cutts. The Scotch footguards marched under the command of their countryman James Douglas. Conspicuous among the Dutch troops were Portland's and Ginkell's Horse, and Solmes's Blue regiment, consisting of two thousand of the finest infantry in Europe. Germany had sent to the field some warriors, sprung from her noblest houses. Prince George of Hesse Darmstadt, a gallant youth, who was serving his apprenticeship in the military art, rode near the King. A strong brigade of Danish mercenaries was commanded by Duke Charles Frederic of Wurtemberg. It was reported that of all the soldiers of William these were most dreaded by the Irish. For centuries of Saxon domination had not effaced the recollection of the violence and cruelty of the Scandinavian sea kings; and an ancient prophecy that the Danes would one day destroy the children of the soil was still repeated with superstitious horror. Among the foreign auxiliaries were a Brandenburg regiment and a Finland regiment. But in that great array, so variously composed, were two bodies of men animated by a spirit peculiarly fierce and implacable, the Huguenots of France thirsting for the blood of the French, and the Englishry of Ireland impatient to trample down the Irish. The ranks of the refugees had been effectually purged of spies and traitors, and were made up of men such as had contended in the preceding century against the power of the House of Valois and the genius of the House of Lorraine. All the boldest spirits of the unconquerable colony had repaired to William's camp. Mitchelburne was there with the stubborn defenders of Londonderry, and Wolseley with the warriors who had raised the unanimous shout of 'Advance' on the day of Newton Butler: Sir Albert Conyngham, the ancester of the noble family whose seat now overlooks the field of battle, had brought from the neighbourhood of Lough Erne a gallant regiment of dragoons which still glories in the name of Enniskillen, and which has proved on the shores of the Euxine that it has not degenerated since the day of the Boyne.

Walker, notwithstanding his advanced age and his peaceful profession, accompanied the men of Londonderry, and tried to animate their zeal by exhortation and by example. He was now a great prelate. Ezekiel Hopkins had taken refuge from Popish persecutors and Presbyterian rebels in the city of London, had brought himself to swear allegiance to the government, had obtained a cure, and had died in the performance of the humble duties of a parish priest. William, on his march through Louth, learned that the rich see of Derry was at his disposal. He instantly made choice of Walker to be the new Bishop. The brave old man, during the few hours of life which remained to him, was overwhelmed with salutations and congratulations. Unhappily he had, during the siege in which he had so highly distinguished himself, contracted a passion for war; and he easily persuaded himself that, in indulging this passion, he was discharging a duty to his country and his religion. He ought to have remembered that the peculiar circumstances which had justified him in becoming a combatant had ceased to exist, and that, in a disciplined army led by generals of long experience and great fame, a fighting divine was likely to give less help than scandal. The Bishop elect was determined to be wherever danger was; and the way in which he exposed himself excited the extreme disgust of his royal patron, who hated a meddler almost as much as a coward. A soldier who ran away from a battle and a gownsman who pushed himself into a battle were the two objects which most strongly excited William's spleen.

It was still early in the day. The King rode slowly along the northern bank of the river, and closely examined the position of the Irish, from whom he was sometimes separated by an interval of little more than two hundred feet. He was accompanied by Schomberg, Ormond, Sidney, Solmes, Prince George of Hesse, Coningsby, and others. 'Their army is but small,' said one of the Dutch officers. Indeed it did not appear to consist of more than sixteen thousand men. But it was well known, from the reports brought by deserters, that many regiments were concealed from view by the undulations of the ground. 'They may be stronger than they look,' said William; 'but, weak or strong, I will soon know all about them.'

At length he alighted at a spot nearly opposite to Oldbridge, sat down on the turf to rest himself, and called for breakfast. The sumpter horses were unloaded : the canteens were opened; and a tablecloth was spread on the grass. The place is marked by an obelisk, built while many veterans who could well remember the events of that day were still living.

While William was at his repast, a group of horsemen appeared close to the water on the opposite shore. Among them his attendants could discern some who had once been conspicuous at reviews in Hyde Park and at balls in the gallery of Whitehall, the youthful Berwick, the small, fairhaired Lauzun, Tyrconnel, once admired by maids of honour as the model of manly vigour and beauty, but now bent down by years and crippled by gout, and, overtopping all, the stately head of Sarsfield.

The chiefs of the Irish army soon discovered that the person who, surrounded by a splendid circle, was breakfasting on the opposite bank, was the Prince of Orange. They sent for artillery. Two field pieces, screened from view by a troop of cavalry, were brought down almost to the brink of the river, and placed behind a hedge. William, who had just risen from his meal, and was again in the saddle, was the mark of both guns. The first shot struck one of the holsters of Prince George of Hesse, and brought his horse to the ground. 'Ah!' cried the King; 'the poor

Prince is killed.' As the words passed his lips, he was himself hit by a second ball, a sixpounder. It merely tore his coat, grazed his shoulder, and drew two or three ounces of blood. Both armies saw that the shot had taken effect; for the King sunk down for a moment on his horse's neck. A yell of exultation rose from the Irish camp. The English and their allies were in dismay. Solmes flung himself prostrate on the earth, and burst into tears. But William's deportment soon reassured his friends. 'There is no harm done,' he said : 'but the bullet came quite near enough.' Coningsby put his handkerchief to the wound : a surgeon was sent for : a plaster was applied; and the King, as soon as the dressing was finished, rode round all the posts of his army amidst loud acclamations. Such was the energy of his spirit that, in spite of his feeble health, in spite of his recent hurt, he was that day nineteen hours on horseback.

A cannonade was kept up on both sides till the evening. William observed with especial attention the effect produced by the Irish shots on the English regiments which had never been in action, and declared himself satisfied with the result. 'All is right,' he said : 'they stand fire well.' Long after sunset he made a final inspection of his forces by torchlight, and gave orders that every thing should be ready for forcing a passage across the river on the morrow. Every soldier was to put a green bough in his hat. The baggage and great coats were to be left under a guard. The word was Westminster.

The King's resolution to attack the Irish was not approved by all his lieutenants. Schomberg, in particular, pronounced the experiment too hazardous, and, when his opinion was over-ruled, retired to his tent in no very good humour. When the order of battle was delivered to him, he muttered that he had been more used to give such orders than to receive them. For this little fit of sullenness, very pardonable in a general who had won great victories when his master was still a child, the brave veteran made, on the following morning, a noble atonement.

The first of July [1690] dawned, a day which has never since returned without exciting strong emotions of very different kinds in the two populations which divide Ireland. The sun rose bright and cloudless. Soon after four both armies were in motion. William ordered his right wing, under the command of Meinhart Schomberg, one of the Duke's sons, to march to the bridge of Slane, some miles up the river, to cross there, and to turn the left flank of the Irish army. Meinhart Schomberg was assisted by Portland and Douglas. James, anticipating some such design, had already sent to the bridge a regiment of dragoons, commanded by Sir Neil O'Neil. O'Neil behaved himself like a brave gentleman: but he soon received a mortal wound: his men fled; and the English right wing passed the river.

This move made Lauzun uneasy. What if the English right wing should get into the rear of the army of James? About four miles south of the Boyne was a place called Duleek, where the road to Dublin was so narrow, that two cars could not pass each other, and where on both sides of the road lay a morass which afforded no firm footing. If Meinhart Schomberg should occupy this spot, it would be impossible for the Irish to retreat. They must either conquer, or be cut off to a man. Disturbed by this apprehension, the French general marched with his countrymen and with Sarsfield's horse in the direction of Slane Bridge. Thus the fords near Oldbridge were left to be defended by the Irish alone.

It was now near ten o'clock. William put himself at the head of his left wing, which was composed exclusively of cavalry, and prepared to pass the river not far above Drogheda. The centre of his army, which consisted almost exclusively of foot, was entrusted to the command of Schomberg, and was marshalled opposite to Oldbridge. At Oldbridge had been collected the whole Irish army, foot, dragoons, and horse, Sarsfield's regiment alone excepted. The Meath bank bristled with pikes and bayonets. A fortification had been made by French engineers out of the hedges and buildings; and a breast work had been thrown up close to the water side. Tyrconnel was there; and under him were Richard Hamilton and Antrim.

Schomberg gave the word. Solmes's Blues were the first to

move. They marched gallantly, with drums beating, to the brink of the Boyne. Then the drums stopped; and the men, ten abreast, descended into the water. Next plunged Londonderry and Enniskillen. A little to the left of Londonderry and Enniskillen, Caillemot crossed, at the head of a long column of French refugees. A little to the left of Caillemot and his refugees, the main body of the English infantry struggled through the river, up to their armpits in water. Still further down the stream the Danes found another ford. In a few minutes the Boyne, for a quarter of a mile, was alive with muskets and green boughs.

It was not till the assailants had reached the middle of the channel that they became aware of the whole difficulty and danger of the service in which they were engaged. They had as yet seen little more than half the hostile army. Now whole regiments of foot and horse seemed to start out of the earth. A wild shout of defiance rose from the whole shore: during one moment the event seemed doubtful: but the Protestants pressed resolutely forward; and in another moment the whole Irish line gave way. Tyrconnel looked on in helpless despair. He did not want personal courage: but his military skill was so small that he hardly ever reviewed his regiment in the Phœnix Park without committing some blunder; and to rally the ranks which were breaking all round him was no task for a general who had survived the energy of his body and of his mind, and yet had still the rudiments of his profession to learn. Several of his best officers fell while vainly endeavouring to prevail on their soldiers to look the Dutch Blues in the face. Richard Hamilton ordered a body of foot to fall on the French refugees, who were still deep in water. He led the way, and, accompanied by some courageous gentlemen, advanced, sword in hand, into the river. But neither his commands nor his example could infuse valour into that mob of cowstealers. He was left almost alone, and retired from the bank in despair. Further down the river, Antrim's division ran like sheep at the approach of the English column. Whole regiments flung away arms, colours and cloaks, and scampered off to the hills without striking a blow or firing a shot.

It required many years and many heroic exploits to take away the reproach which that ignominious rout left on the Irish name. Yet, even before the day closed, it was abundantly proved that the reproach was unjust. Richard Hamilton put himself at the head of the cavalry, and, under his command, they made a gallant, though an unsuccessful attempt to retrieve the day. They maintained a desperate fight in the bed of the river with Solmes's Blues. They drove the Danish brigade back into the stream. They fell impetuously on the Huguenot regiments, which, not being provided with pikes, then ordinarily used by foot to repel horse, began to give ground. Caillemot, while encouraging his fellow exiles, received a mortal wound in the thigh. Four of his men carried him back across the ford to his tent. As he passed, he continued to urge forward the rear ranks which were still up to the breast in the water. 'On; on; my lads! to glory! to glory!' Schomberg, who had remained on the northern bank, and who had thence watched the progress of his troops with the eye of a general, now thought that the emergency required from him the personal exertion of a soldier. Those who stood about him besought him in vain to put on his cuirass. Without defensive armour he rode through the river, and rallied the refugees whom the fall of Caillemot had dismayed. 'Come on,' he cried in French, pointing to the Popish squadrons; 'come on, gentlemen : there are your persecutors.' Those were his last words. As he spoke, a band of Irish horsemen rushed upon him and encircled him for a moment. When they retired, he was on the ground. His friends raised him; but he was already a corpse. Two sabre wounds were on his head; and a bullet from a carbine was lodged in his neck. Almost at the same moment Walker, while exhorting the colonists of Ulster to play the men, was shot dead. During near half an hour the battle continued to rage along the southern shore of the river. All was smoke, dust and din. Old soldiers were heard to say that they had seldom seen sharper work in the Low Countries. But, just at this conjuncture, William came up with the left wing. He had found much difficulty in crossing. The tide was running fast. His charger had been forced to swim, and had been almost lost in the mud. As soon as the King was on firm ground he took his sword in his left hand,—for his right arm was stiff with his wound and his bandage,—and led his men to the place where the fight was the hottest. His arrival decided the fate of the day. Yet the Irish horse retired fighting obstinately. It was long remembered among the Protestants of Ulster that, in the midst of the tumult, William rode to the head of the Enniskilleners. 'What will you do for me?' he cried. He was not immediately recognised; and one trooper, taking him for an enemy, was about to fire. William gently put aside the carbine. 'What,' said he, 'do you not know your friends?' 'It is His Majesty,' said the Colonel. The ranks of sturdy Protestant yeomen set up a shout of joy. 'Gentlemen,' said William, 'you shall be my guards to day. I have heard much of you. Let me see something of you.' One of the most remarkable peculiarities of this man, ordinarily so saturnine and reserved, was that danger acted on him like wine, opened his heart, loosened his tongue, and took away all appearance of constraint from his manner. On this memorable day he was seen wherever the peril was greatest. One ball struck the cap of his pistol: another carried off the heel of his jackboot: but his lieutenants in vain implored him to retire to some station from which he could give his orders without exposing a life so valuable to Europe. His troops, animated by his example, gained ground fast. The Irish cavalry made their last stand at a house called Plottin Castle, about a mile and a half south of Oldbridge. There the Enniskilleners were repelled with the loss of fifty men, and were hotly pursued, till William rallied them and turned the chase back. In this encounter Richard Hamilton, who had done all that could be done by valour to retrieve a reputation forfeited by perfidy,[1] was severely wounded, taken prisoner, and instantly brought, through the smoke and over the carnage, before the prince whom he had foully wronged. On no occasion did the character of William show itself in a more striking manner. 'Is

---

[1] [Richard Hamilton had been sent over to Ireland on parole by William. But he had broken his word and become one of James's generals.]

this business over?' he said; 'or will your horse make more fight?' 'On my honour, Sir,' answered Hamilton, 'I believe that they will.' 'Your honour!' muttered William; 'your honour!' That half suppressed exclamation was the only revenge which he condescended to take for an injury for which many sovereigns, far more affable and gracious in their ordinary deportment, would have exacted a terrible retribution. Then, restraining himself, he ordered his own surgeon to look to the hurts of the captive.

And now the battle was over. Hamilton was mistaken in thinking that his horse would continue to fight. Whole troops had been cut to pieces. One fine regiment had only thirty un-wounded men left. It was enough that these gallant soldiers had disputed the field till they were left without support, or hope, or guidance, till their bravest leader was a captive, and till their King had fled.

3. HISTORY OF ENGLAND: THE DEATH OF WILLIAM III

Meanwhile reports about the state of the King's health were constantly becoming more and more alarming. His medical advisers, both English and Dutch, were at the end of their resources. He had consulted by letter all the most eminent physicians of Europe; and, as he was apprehensive that they might return flattering answers if they knew who he was, he had written under feigned names. To Fagon he had described himself as a parish priest. Fagon replied, somewhat bluntly, that such symptoms could have only one meaning, and that the only advice which he had to give to the sick man was to prepare himself for death. Having obtained this plain answer, William consulted Fagon again without disguise, and obtained some prescriptions which were thought to have a little retarded the approach of the inevitable hour. But the great King's days were numbered. Headaches and shivering fits returned on him almost daily. He still rode and even hunted; but he had no longer that firm seat or that perfect command of the bridle for which he had once been renowned. Still all his care was for the future. The filial respect and tenderness of Albemarle had been almost a necessary of life to him. But it was of importance that Heinsius should be fully informed both as to the whole plan for the next campaign and as to the state of the preparations. Albemarle was in full possession of the King's views on these subjects. He was therefore sent to the Hague. Heinsius was at that time suffering from indisposition, which was indeed a trifle when compared with the maladies under which William was sinking. But in the nature of William there was none of that selfishness which is the too common vice of invalids. On the twentieth of February he sent to Heinsius a letter in which he did not even allude to his own sufferings and infirmities. 'I am,' he said, 'infinitely concerned to learn that your health is not yet quite reestablished. May God be pleased to grant you a speedy recovery. I am unalterably your good friend, William.' Those were the last lines of that long correspondence.

On the twentieth of February William was ambling on a favourite horse, named Sorrel, through the park of Hampton Court. He urged his horse to strike into a gallop just at the spot where a mole had been at work. Sorrel stumbled on the mole-hill, and went down on his kness. The King fell off, and broke his collar bone. The bone was set; and he returned to Kensington in his coach. The jolting of the rough roads of that time made it necessary to reduce the fracture again. To a young and vigorous man such an accident would have been a trifle. But the frame of William was not in a condition to bear even the slightest shock. He felt that his time was short, and grieved, with a grief such as only noble spirits feel, to think that he must leave his work but half finished. It was possible that he might still live until one of his plans should be carried into execution. He had long known that the relation in which England and Scotland stood to each other was at best precarious, and often unfriendly, and that it might be doubted whether, in an estimate of the British power, the resources of the smaller country ought not to be deducted from those of the larger.

Recent events had proved that, without doubt, the two kingdoms could not possibly continue for another year to be on the terms on which they had been during the preceding century, and that there must be between them either absolute union or deadly enmity. Their enmity would bring frightful calamities, not on themselves alone, but on all the civilized world. Their union would be the best security for the prosperity of both, for the internal tranquillity of the island, for the just balance of power among European states, and for the immunities of all Protestant countries. On the twenty-eighth of February the Commons listened with uncovered heads to the last message that bore William's sign manual. An unhappy accident, he told them, had forced him to make to them in writing a communication which he would gladly have made from the throne. He had, in the first year of his reign expressed his desire to see an union accomplished between England and Scotland. He was convinced that nothing could more conduce to the safety and happiness of both. He should think it his peculiar felicity if, before the close of his reign, some happy expedient could be devised for making the two kingdoms one; and he, in the most earnest manner, recommended the question to the consideration of the Houses. It was resolved that the message should be taken into consideration on Saturday, the seventh of March.

But on the first of March humours of menacing appearance showed themselves in the king's knee. On the fourth of March he was attacked by fever; on the fifth his strength failed greatly; and on the sixth he was scarcely kept alive by cordials. The Abjuration Bill and a money bill were awaiting his assent. That assent he felt that he should not be able to give in person. He therefore ordered a commission to be prepared for his signature. His hand was now too weak to form the letters of his name, and it was suggested that a stamp should be prepared. On the seventh of March the stamp was ready. The Lord Keeper and the clerks of the parliament came, according to usage, to witness the signing of the commission. But they were detained some hours in the antechamber while he was in one of the paroxysms of his malady. Meanwhile the Houses were sitting. It was

Saturday, the seventh, the day on which the Commons had resolved to take into consideration the question of the union with Scotland. But that subject was not mentioned. It was known that the King had but a few hours to live; and the members asked each other anxiously whether it was likely that the Abjuration and money bills would be passed before he died. After sitting long in the expectation of a message, the Commons adjourned till six in the afternoon. By that time William had recovered himself sufficiently to put the stamp on the parchment which authorized his commissioners to act for him. In the evening, when the Houses had assembled, Black Rod knocked. The Commons were summoned to the bar of the Lords; the commission was read, the Abjuration Bill and the Malt Bill became laws, and both Houses adjourned till nine o'clock in the morning of the following day. The following day was Sunday. But there was little chance that William would live through the night. It was of the highest importance that, within the shortest possible time after his decease, the successor designated by the Bill of Rights and the Act of Succession should receive the homage of the Estates of the Realm, and be publicly proclaimed in the Council: and the most rigid Pharisee in the Society for the Reformation of Manners could hardly deny that it was lawful to save the state, even on the Sabbath.

The King meanwhile was sinking fast. Albemarle had arrived at Kensington from the Hague, exhausted by rapid travelling. His master kindly bade him go to rest for some hours, and then summoned him to make his report. That report was in all respects satisfactory. The States General were in the best temper; the troops, the provisions and the magazines were in the best order. Every thing was in readiness for an early campaign. William received the intelligence with the calmness of a man whose work was done. He was under no illusion as to his danger. 'I am fast drawing,' he said, 'to my end.' His end was worthy of his life. His intellect was not for a moment clouded. His fortitude was the more admirable because he was not willing to die. He had very lately said to one of those whom he most loved: 'You know that I never feared death; there have been times when I should have wished it; but, now that this great new prospect is opening before me, I do wish to stay here a little longer.' Yet no weakness, no querulousness, disgraced the noble close of that noble career. To the physicians the King returned his thanks graciously and gently. 'I know that you have done all that skill and learning could do for me : but the case is beyond your art; and I submit.' From the words which escaped him he seemed to be frequently engaged in mental prayer. Burnet and Tenison remained many hours in the sick room. He professed to them his firm belief in the truth of the Christian religion, and received the sacrament from their hands with great seriousness. The antechambers were crowded all night with lords and privy councillors. He ordered several of them to be called in, and exerted himself to take leave of them with a few kind and cheerful words. Among the English who were admitted to his bedside were Devonshire and Ormond. But there were in the crowd those who felt as no Englishman could feel, friends of his youth who had been true to him, and to whom he had been true, through all vicissitudes of fortune; who had served him with unalterable fidelity when his Secretaries of State, his Treasury and his Admiralty had betrayed him; who had never on any field of battle, or in an atmosphere tainted with loathsome and deadly disease, shrunk from placing their own lives in jeopardy to save his, and whose truth he had at the cost of his own popularity rewarded with bounteous munificence. He strained his feeble voice to thank Auverquerque for the affectionate and loyal services of thirty years. To Albermarle he gave the keys of his closet, and of his private drawers. 'You know,' he said, 'what to do with them.' By this time he could scarcely respire. 'Can this,' he said to the physicians, 'last long ?' He was told that the end was approaching. He swallowed a cordial, and asked for Bentinck. Those were his last articulate words. Bentinck instantly came to the bedside, bent down, and placed his ear close to the King's mouth. The lips of the dying man moved; but nothing could be heard. The King took the hand of his earliest friend, and pressed it tenderly to his heart. In that moment, no doubt, all that had cast a slight passing cloud over their long and pure friendship was forgotten. It was now between seven and eight in the morning. He closed his eyes, and gasped for breath. The bishops knelt down and read the commendatory prayer. When it ended William was no more.

When his remains were laid out, it was found that he wore next to his skin a small piece of black silk riband. The lords in waiting ordered it to be taken off. It contained a gold ring and a lock of the hair of Mary.

Bibliographical Note

WITHOUT the aid of the house of Trevelyan, this little book could not have been written. To the late Sir George Otto Trevelyan I owe the guidance of the most brilliant and authoritative of Victorian biographies, *The Life and Letters of Lord Macaulay*, and to his son, the late Dr G. M. Trevelyan, the permission to use the letters and private journals of Macaulay (now in the Library of Trinity College, Cambridge) from which that work was largely compiled. I have thus been enabled to embody material which Sir G. O. Trevelyan, writing in the lifetime of many of Macaulay's contemporaries, could not use. To G. M. Trevelyan I also owed the most generous personal help and criticism, and to him and his brother, the late Sir Charles Trevelyan, the privilege of studing the marginal notes, with which Macaulay enriched his books.

A list of authorities consulted follows. The most important are marked by an asterisk. I have also added the more important works on Macaulay published since 1932, including the six volumes – two still to be published – of Professor Thomas Pinney's magnificent edition of Macaulay's *Letters*.

A. MACAULAY'S OWN WRITINGS AND LETTERS

1. *Manuscripts.*
    *Macaulay's Journals, 1838–9, 1848–59. 11 vols.
    *Letters of Macaulay to Thomas Flower Ellis.
        (Both the above are in the Library of Trinity College, Cam-

bridge, where they have been placed by their former owner, Professor G. M. Trevelyan.)

*Miscellaneous Letters of Macaulay's formerly in the possession of Professor G. M. Trevelyan at Hallington Hall, Northumberland.

*Macaulay's marginal notes in the volumes of his Library, formerly in the possession of the Rt Hon. Sir Charles Trevelyan, Bart, of Wallington Hall, Northumberland, and Professor G. M. Trevelyan of Hallington Hall.

2. *Printed Works.*

(a) *Separate First Editions.*

Pompeii (prize poem). 1819.

Evening (prize poem). 1821.

Lays of Ancient Rome. 1842. ['Ivry', first published in *Knight's Quarterly Magazine*, and 'The Armada', first published in *Friendship's Offering*, added in 1848 ed.]

Critical and Historical Essays contributed to the Edinburgh Review. 3 vols. 1843.

History of England.

Vols. i. and ii. 1848.

Vols. iii. and iv. 1855.

Vol. v. (ed. Lady Trevelyan). 1861.

Inaugural Address (as Lord Rector of Glasgow). 1849.

Speeches Corrected by Himself. 1854. (An unathorized edition had been published by Vizetelly in 1853.)

Lees, W. N. *Indian Musalmáns.* [Macaulay's Minute.] 1857.

Miscellaneous Writings (ed. T. F. Ellis) [including contributions to the *Encyclopædia Britannica*, *Knight's Quarterly Magazine*, and early contributions to the *Edinburgh Review*]. 2 vols. 1860.

*Woodrow, H. *The Indian Education Minutes of Lord Macaulay.* Calcutta, 1862.

*Laurie, W. F. B. *Sketches of Some Distinguished Anglo-Indians.* [Lord Macaulay's Great Minute on Education.] 1888.

*Trevelyan, Sir G. O. *The Marginal Notes of Lord Macaulay.* 1907.

(b) *Collected Works.*

The Works of Lord Macaulay (ed. Lady Trevelyan). 8 vols. 1866.

The Works of Lord Macaulay (Albany ed.). 12 vols. 1898.

3. *Printed Letters of Macaulay.*

Arnould, Sir J. *Memoirs of Thomas, 1st Lord Denman,* vol. ii. 1873.

Arundell of Wardour, Lord. *Some Papers of.* 1909.

Charnwood, Lady, *An Autograph Collection.* 1930.

Fagan, L. *Life of Sir Anthony Panizzi,* vol. i. 1880.

Hodder, E. *Life and Works of the 7th Earl of Shaftesbury,* vol. iii. 1886.

*Macaulay, *The Letters of Thomas Babington* (ed. Thomas Pinney).

    Vol. i. 1807–February 1831. 1974.

    Vol. ii. March 1831–December 1833. 1974.

    Vol. iii. January 1834–August 1841. 1976.

    Vol. iv. September 1841–December 1848. 1977.

    Vol. v. January 1849–December 1853.

    Vol. vi. January 1854–December 1859.

Mackie, J. B. *Life and Work of Duncan M'Laren,* vol. i. 1888.

More, Hannah. *Letters of Hannah More to Zachary Macaulay* (ed. A. Roberts). 1860.

Morley, John. *Life of Gladstone,* vol. ii. 1903.

Morrison, Alfred. *The Manuscripts of* (Appendix to the Ninth Report of the Royal Commission on Historical Manuscripts). 1883.

*Napier, Macvey. *Selections from the Correspondence of.* 1879.

Russell, Lord John. *The Later Correspondence of* (ed. G. P. Gooch). 2 vols. 1925.

Taylor, Henry. *Correspondence of* (ed. E. Dowson). 1888.

*Trevelyan, Sir G. O. *Life and Letters of Lord Macaulay* [for numerous extracts from Macaulay's journals and correspondence]. 2 vols. 1876, 1877, 1878, 1881, 1908, 1932.

B. Biography and Criticism

Arnold, Rev. F. *The Public Life of Lord Macaulay.* 1862.

Arnold, Matthew. *On the Study of Celtic Literature.* [On Translating Homer.] 1867.

Arnold, Matthew. *Mixed Essays.* [A French Critic on Milton.] 1879.

Avebury, Lord. *Essays and Addresses.* [Macaulay.] 1903.

Babington, C. *Macaulay's Character of the Clergy in the Seventeenth Century Considered.* 1849.

*Bagehot, W. *Literary Studies,* vol. ii. [Thomas Babington Macaulay.] 1879.

Balfour, A. J., 1st Earl of. *Chapters of Autobiography*. 1930.

Canning, Hon. A. S. G. *Lord Macaulay, Essayist and Historian*. 1882.

*Clive, J. L., *Macaulay, The Shaping of the Historian*. 1973.

Croker, J. W. *Quarterly Review*, March 1849. [*The History of England*.]

Crozier, J. B. *My Inner Life*. 1898.

Dixon, W. H. *Life of Penn*. [The Macaulay Charges.] 1851.

Firth, C. H. *Commentary on Macaulay's History of England*. 1928.

Forster, W. E. Preface to 1849 ed. of *Clarkson's Memoirs of Penn*.

Gay, Peter. *Style in History*. 1975.

*Gladstone, W. E. *Gleanings from Past Years*. [Macaulay.] 1879.

*Hamburger, J. *Macaulay and the Whig Tradition*. 1976.

*Harrison, Frederic. *Studies in Early Victorian Literature*. [Lord Macaulay.] 1895.

Impey, E. B. *Memorials of Sir Elijah Impey*. 1846.

*Jebb, Sir R. C. *Macaulay*. 1900.

Levine, G. L. *Boundaries of Fiction*. 1968.

Lockhart, J. G. *Answers to Macaulay's Criticism of Croker's Boswell*. 1856.

*Macgregor, D. H. *Lord Macaulay*. 1901.

Martineau, Harriet. *Biographical Sketches*. [Macaulay.] 1869.

*Millgate, E. J. *Macaulay*. 1973.

*Milman, H. H. *Memoir of Macaulay* (in vol. vii. of 1858–62 ed. of Macaulay's *History of England*).

*Montague, F. C. *Macaulay's Essays*. [Introduction and Notes.] 3 vols. 1903.

*Morison, J. Cotter. *Macaulay*. (English Men of Letters.) 1882.

*Morley, John. *Miscellaneous Studies*, vol. i. [Macaulay.] 1886.

*Mumby, A. N. L. *Macaulay's Library*. 1966.

Oursel, P. *Les Essais de Lord Macaulay*. 1882.

*Paget, J. *The New Examen*. 1861. (Republished in *Paradoxes and Puzzles*, 1874.) 1934.

*Pattison, Mark. *Encyclopædia Britannica*. [Macaulay.]

*Paul, H. *Men and Letters*. [Macaulay and his Critics.] 1901.

Ponsonby, A. *English Diaries*. 1923.

Quick, R. H. *Life and Remains*. [Macaulay's *Johnson*.] 1899.

*Roberts, S. C. *Lord Macaulay*. (Engl. Assoc. Pamphlet No. 67.) 1927.

*St. Aubyn, G. *Macaulay*. 1952.

*Saintsbury, George. *Corrected Impressions.* [Macaulay.] 1895.

*Saintsbury, George. *Cambridge History of English Literature,* vol. xiii. [Lesser Poets of the Middle and Later Nineteenth Century.]

[Skelton, Sir J.]. *Nugae Criticae.* [The Whig Historian.] 1862.

Spedding, J. *Evenings with a Reviewer.* 1881.

Stanhope, Earl. *Lord John Russell and Mr. Macaulay on the French Revolution.* 1833.

Stephen, Sir J. F. *The Story of Nuncomar.* 1885.

*Stephen, Leslie. *Hours in a Library,* vol. iii. [Macaulay.] 1879.

*Stephen, Leslie. *D. of N.B.* [Macaulay.]

Stirling, J. H. *Jerrold, Tennyson and Macaulay.* 1868.

*[Thackeray, W. M.] *Cornhill,* March 1860. [A Few Words on Junius and Macaulay.]

Thackeray, W. M. *Stray Papers.* [Mr. Macaulay's *Essays.*] 1901.

*Trevelyan, G. M. *Clio: A Muse.* 1913, 1930, 1931.

*Trevelyan, Sir G. O. *Life and Letters of Lord Macaulay.* 2 vols. 1876, 1877, 1878, 1881, 1908, 1932.

*Trevelyan, Sir G. O. *The Marginal Notes of Lord Macaulay.* 1907.

Walker, H. *Cambridge Modern History,* vol. xi. [English Literature, 1840–70.]

Ward, Sir A. W. *Cambridge History of English Literature,* vol. xiv. [Historians, Biographers and Political Orators.]

Wotton, Mabel. *Word Portraits of Famous Writers.* [Macaulay.] 1887.

Young, C. K. *Macaulay.* 1977.

C. Contemporary Allusions to Macaulay

Abbott, E., and Campbell, L. *Life and Letters of Benjamin Jowett,* vol. i. 1897.

Airlie, Mabel, Countess of. *Lord Palmerston and his Times,* vol. i. 1922.

Argyll, Duke of. *Passages from the Past.* 2 vols. 1907.

Argyll, George Douglas, Duke of. *Autobiography and Memoirs* (ed. Duchess of Argyll). 2 vols. 1906.

Arnould, Sir J. *Memoirs of Thomas, 1st Lord Denman.* 2 vols. 1873.

Arundell of Wardour, Lord. *Some Papers of.* 1909.

Ashley, Hon. E. *Life and Correspondence of Henry John Temple, Viscount Palmerston.* 2 vols. 1879.

Ashwell, A. R., and Wilberforce, R. *Life of Samuel Wilberforce,* vols. i. and ii. 1880.

Bancroft, Elizabeth. *Letters from England.* 1904.

Bancroft, F. *Life and Works of William H. Seward,* vol. i. 1900.

Bancroft, G. *Life and Letters of* (ed. M. A. De Wolfe Howe), vol. ii. New York, 1908.

Berry, Miss. *Extracts from the Journal and Correspondence of* (ed. Lady Theresa Lewis), vol. iii. 1865.

Blount, Sir E. *Memoirs.* 1902.

Bright, John. *The Diaries of.* 1930.

Brookfield, Charles and Francis. *Mrs. Brookfield and her Circle.* 1905.

Brougham, Lord. *Life and Times of Henry, Lord Brougham,* vol. iii. 1871.

Broughton, Lord. *Recollections of a Long Life.* Vols. v. and vi. 1911.

Buckingham, Duke of. *Memoirs of Courts and Cabinets of William IV. and Victoria.* 2 vols. 1861.

Buckley, K. *Joseph Parkes of Birmingham.* [1926.]

Butler, J. R. *Passing of the Great Reform Bill.* 1914.

Byrne, Mrs Pitt. *Gossip of the Century,* vol. i. 1892.

Carlyle, Thomas. *New Letters of* (ed. A. Carlyle), vol. ii. 1904.

Clark, J. W. *Life and Letters of the Rev. Adam Sedgwick.* 2 vols. 1890.

Cockburn, Lord. *Life of Lord Jeffrey.* 2 vols. 1852.

Cockburn, Lord. *Journal, 1831–54.* 2 vols. 1874.

Colebrooke, Sir T. E. *Life of the Honourable Mountstuart Elphinstone,* vol. ii. 1884.

Coleridge, Sara. *Memoirs and Letters of.* 2 vols. 1873.

Cook, Sir E. *Life of Florence Nightingale,* vol. i. 1914.

Coupland, R. *Wilberforce.* 1923.

Creevey, T. *The Creevey Papers* (ed. Sir H. Maxwell), vol. ii. 1903.

Croker, J. W. *Correspondence and Diaries of* (ed. L. J. Jennings), vol. ii. 1884.

Darwin, Charles. *Life and Letters of* (ed. F. Darwin), vol. i. 1887.

Darwin, Emma. *A Century of Family Letters.* 2 vols. 1915.

Dasent, A. W. *John Theophilus Delane.* 2 vols. 1908.

Dudley, 1st Earl of. *Letters to Ivy* (ed. S. H. Romilly). 1905.

Duff, Sir M. Grant. *Notes from a Diary, 1851–72,* vol. i. 1897.

Eastlake, Lady. *Journals and Correspondence of* (ed. C. E. Smith), vol. i. 1895.

Eden, Miss. *Letters* (ed. Violet Dickinson). 1919.

Ellenborough, Lord. *A Political Diary* (ed. E. Law), vol. ii. 1881.

Emerson, R. W. *Journals of*, vol. vii. 1913.

Fagan, L. *Life of Sir Anthony Panizzi.* 2 vols. 1880.

Fawcett, M. G. *What I Remember.* [1924.]

Fitzmaurice, Lord E. *Life of 2nd Earl Granville*, vol. i. 1905.

Froude, J. A. *Thomas Carlyle, 1795–1834*, vol. ii. 1882.

Froude, J. A. *Thomas Carlyle, 1834–81*, vol. i. 1884.

Gaussen, A. C. C. *A Later Pepys*, vol. ii. 1904.

Gordon, Mrs. *Christopher North: A Memoir of John Wilson.* 1862.

Granville, Harriet, Countess of. *Letters, 1810–45*, vol. ii. 1894.

Greville, Charles. *The Greville Memoirs (George IV and William IV)*, vols. ii. and iii. 1874, 1888.

Greville, Charles. *The Greville Memoirs (Victoria)*, vols. i. and ii. 1885, 1888.

Hall, S. C. *Retrospect of a Long Life*, vol. i. 1883.

Hansard. *Parliamentary Debates.*

Hare, A. J. C. *The Gurneys of Earlham*, vol. ii. 1895.

Hare, A. J. C. *The Story of My Life*, vols. i, iv., vi. 1896.

Hawthorne, Julian. *Nathaniel Hawthorne and his Wife*, vol. ii. 1885.

Hayward, Abraham. *A Selection from the Correspondence of* (ed. H. E. Carlisle). 2 vols. 1886.

Hill, Sir R., and G. B. *Life of Sir Rowland Hill*, 2 vols. 1880.

Hill, R., and F. D. *A Memoir of Matthew Davenport Hill.* 1878.

Hodder, E. *Life and Works of the 7th Earl of Shaftesbury*, vols. ii. and iii. 1886.

Holland, Lady. *A Memoir of the Rev. Sydney Smith.* 2 vols. 1855.

Howe, M. A. De Wolfe. *James Ford Rhodes.* New York, 1929.

Irving, P. M. *Life and Letters of Washington Irving*, vol. iv. New York. 1864.

Kaye, J. W. *Life and Correspondence of Charles, Lord Metcalfe*, vol. ii. 1854.

Knight, Charles. *Passages of a Working Life.* 3 vols. 1863.

Lang, Andrew. *Life and Letters of John Gibson Lockhart*, vol. ii. 1897.

Le Marchant, Sir D. *Memoir of Lord Althorp.* 1876.

Lee-Warner, Sir W. *Life of the Marquis of Dalhousie.* 2 vols. 1904.

Lewis, Sir George. *Letters of* (ed. Sir G. F. Lewis). 1870.

Lieven, Princess, and Earl Grey. *Correspondence of* (ed. G. Le Strange), vol. ii. 1890.

Login, E. D. *Lady Login's Recollections*. 1916.

Lyell, Sir Charles. *Life, Letters and Journals of* (ed. Mrs Lyell), vol. ii. 1881.

Lytton, Earl of. *Life of Edward Bulwer, 1st Lord Lytton*. 2 vols. 1913.

Lytton, Lady Bulwer. *Unpublished Letters to A. E. Challon*. 1914.

Mackie, J. B. *Life and Work of Duncan M'Laren*, vol. i. 1888.

Marston, E. *After Work*. 1904.

Martin, Sir A. P. *Life and Letters of the Rt. Hon. Robert Lowe, Viscount Sherbrooke*, vol. ii. 1893.

Martin, Sir Theodore. *Life of the Prince Consort*, vols. i. and ii. 1875.

Martineau, Harriet. *History of England during the Thirty Years' Peace*. 2 vols. 1849–50.

Melbourne, Lord. *Papers* (ed. L. C. Sanders). 1889.

Melville, Lewis. *Life of William Makepeace Thackeray*. 2 vols. 1899.

Mill, J. S. *Autobiography*. 1867; New York, 1924.

Mill, J. S. *Letters of* (ed. H. S. R. Elliot). 2 vols. 1910.

Milman, A. *Henry Hart Milman*. 1900.

Milner, Mary. *Life of Isaac Milner*. 1844.

Mitford, Mary Russell. *Correspondence of* (ed. Elizabeth Lee). [1914.]

Mitford, Mary Russell. *Life of* (ed. Rev. A. G. L'Estrange). 3 vols. 1870.

Montgomery, James. *Memoirs of* (ed. J. Holland and J. Everett), vol. vi. 1856.

Monypenny, W. F., and Buckle, G. E. *Life of Benjamin Disraeli, Earl of Beaconsfield*, vols. i–iii. 1910–14.

More, Hannah. *Memoirs of the Life and Correspondence of* (ed. W. Roberts), vol. iv. 1835.

More, Hannah. *Letters of Hannah More to Zachary Macaulay* (ed. A. Roberts). 1860.

Moore, Thomas. *Memoirs, Journal and Correspondence of* (ed. Lord John Russell), vols. vi. and vii. 1856.

Morley, John. *The Life of William Ewart Gladstone*. 3 vols. 1903.

Motley, J. L. *Correspondence of* (ed. G. W. Curtis), vol. i. 1889.

Moultrie, J. *Poems*. 1876.

Napier, Macvey. *Selections from the Correspondence of* (eds. Sir G. Douglas and Sir G. Ramsay). 1879.

O'Brien, Hon. G. *Reminiscences of the Rt. Hon. Lord O'Brien.* 1916.

Owen, Rev. R. *Life of Richard Owen,* vol. i. 1894.

Paget, Sir James. *Memoirs and Letters of* (ed. Stephen Paget). 1901.

Panmure, Lord. *Panmure Papers,* vol. ii. 1898.

Parker, C. S. *Private Papers of Sir Robert Peel,* vols. ii. and iii. 1899.

Parker, C. S. *Life and Letters of Sir James Graham.* 2 vols. 1907.

Pierce, E. L. *Memoirs and Letters of Charles Sumner.* 2 vols. 1878.

Prothero, R. E. *Life and Correspondence of Arthur Penrhyn Stanley,* vol. i. 1893.

Raikes, H. St John. *Life and Letters of Henry Cecil Raikes.* 1898.

Redesdale, Lord. *Memories,* vol. i. 1915.

Reid, S. J. *Life and Letters of the First Earl of Durham.* 2 vols. 1906.

Reid, Sir T. W. *Life, Letters and Friendships of Monckton Milnes, 1st Lord Houghton.* 2 vols. 1890.

Ritchie, G. *The Ritchies in India.* 1920.

Robinson, Major-Gen. C. W. *Life of Sir John Beverley Robinson.* 1904.

Robinson, Henry Crabb. *Diary, Reminiscences and Correspondence,* vols. ii. and iii. 1869.

Roebuck, J. A. *History of the Whig Ministry of 1830.* 2 vols. 1852.

Russell, A., and MacCarthy, D. *Lady John Russell.* 1910.

Russell, Sir E. *That Reminds Me.* 1899.

Russell, G. W. E. *Collections and Recollections.* 1895.

Russell, Lord John. *Early Correspondence of* (ed. Rollo Russell). 2 vols. 1913.

Russell, Lord John. *Later Correspondence of* (ed. G. P. Gooch). 2 vols. 1925.

Shee, W. A. *My Contemporaries.* 1893.

Sidgwick, A. and E. M. *Henry Sidgwick: A Memoir.* 1906.

Smiles, Samuel. *Memoirs and Correspondence of John Murray,* vol. ii. 1891.

Smith, George. *Life of Albert Duff,* vol. ii. 1879.

Smith, George. *Life of John Wilson.* 1878.

Smith, Goldwin. *Reminiscences* (ed. A. Haultain). 1910.

Stephen, Sir James. *Essays in Ecclesiastical Biography.* [The Clapham Sect.] 1849.

Stephen, Sir James. *Letters.* 1906.

Stephen, Leslie. *Life of Sir James Fitzjames Stephen*, 1895.

Stirling, A. M. W. *Life's Little Day*. [1924.]

Stowe, C. E. *Life of Harriet Beecher Stowe*. 1889.

Taylor, Henry. *Autobiography*. 2 vols. 1885.

Teignmouth, Lord. *Reminiscences of Many Years*. 2 vols. Edinburgh, 1878.

Tennyson, 2nd Lord. *Alfred, Lord Tennyson*, vol. i. 1897.

Thackeray, W. M. *A Collection of Letters of, 1847–55*. 1887.

Thirlwall, C. *Letters to a Friend* (ed. Dean Stanley). 1881.

Thornton, P. M. *Some Things we have Remembered*. 1912.

Ticknor, George. *Life, Letters and Journals of*, vol. ii. Boston, 1876.

Torrens, W. M. *Memoirs of William, 2nd Viscount Melbourne*, vol. ii. 1878.

Trevelyan, G. M. *Lord Grey of the Reform Bill* [Appendix H]. 1919.

Trevelyan, G. M. *Sir George Otto Trevelyan*. 1932.

Trollope, T. A. *What I Remember*, vol. ii. 1887.

Twistleton, Hon. Mrs Edward. *Letters of*. 1928.

Walpole, Spencer. *Life of Lord John Russell*. 2 vols. 1889.

Ward, D. C. H. *A Romance of the Nineteenth Century*. 1923.

Ward, W. *Life and Times of Cardinal Wiseman*. 1897.

West, Sir Algernon. *Recollections*. 2 vols. 1899.

Wilberforce, R. I. and S. *Life of William Wilberforce*, vol. v. 1838.

William IV. and Earl Grey. *Correspondence of* (ed. Henry, Earl Grey.) 2 vols. 1867.

Victoria, Queen. *Letters of, 1837–61* (eds. A. C. Benson and Viscount Esher). 3 vols. 1907.

Index